Image of India
in the Indian Novel in English
1960-1985

Image of India
in the Indian Novel in English
1960-1985

Edited by

Sudhakar Pandey
and
R. Raj Rao

[signature: Amrik Singh]

*For Amritjit,
with best wishes
Raj Rao
Pune
January '99.*

Orient Longman

ORIENT LONGMAN LIMITED

Registered Office
3-6-272 Himayatnagar, Hyderabad 500 029

Other Offices
Kamani Marg, Ballard Estate, Bombay 400 038
17 Chittaranjan Avenue, Calcutta 700 072
160 Anna Salai, Madras 600 002
1/24 Asaf Ali Road, New Delhi 110 002
80/1 Mahatma Gandhi Road, Bangalore 560 001
3-6-272 Himayatnagar, Hyderbad 500 029
Birla Mandir Road, Patna 800 004
S.C. Goswami Road, Panbazar, Guwahati 781 001
House no. 28/31, 15 Ashok Marg, Lucknow 226 001
Plot no 205-A, Saheed Nagar, Bhubaneswar 751 007

© Orient Longman Limited 1993
ISBN 0 86311 347 8

Phototypeset in Galliard Roman by
Trendz Phototypesetters, Bombay 400 001

Printed in India at
Hi-Tech Printing Services, Bombay 400 010

Published by Orient Longman Limited,
Kamani Marg, Bombay 400 038

Notes on the Contributors • vii
Introduction •xi

K R SHIRWADKAR
Literature as ideology :
Raja Rao's *The Serpent and the Rope* — 1

V M MADGE
Rise of the demos :
A study of Malgonkar's *The Princes* — 12

R S SINGH
West meets East :
A study of Kamala Markandaya's *Possession* — 21

KALPANA WANDREKAR
The ailing aliens :
Anita Desai's *Bye Bye Blackbird*
as a symptomatic study in schizophrenia — 36

R K DHAWAN
Destiny of a nation :
Arun Joshi's *The Apprentice* — 51

RAMESH DNYATE
The hothouse cactus :
A note on R.K. Narayan's *The Painter of Signs*   61

MAKARAND PARANJAPE
Critique of Communism in
Raja Rao's *Comrade Kirillov*   69

SHIRISH V CHINDHADE
The triumph of timeless India :
Rama Mehta's *Inside the Haveli*   84

VASANT A SHAHANE
Fictional montage in
Anita Desai's *Fire on the Mountain*   92

VRINDA NABAR
The four-dimensional reality :
Anita Desai's *Clear Light of Day*   102

O P MATHUR
A metaphor of reality :
A study of the protagonist of
Midnight's Children   113

VINEY KIRPAL
The perfect bubble :
A study of Anita Desai's *In Custody*   123

NISSIM EZEKIEL
An image of India in
Shouri Daniels' *A City of Children*   135

Index • 141

Notes on the Contributors

K R Shirwadkar has authored books in Marathi on Shakespeare and on Marxist views of literature. He has co-edited *Comparative Studies in Literature and Language* and has recently published a book on the *Indian Novel in English and Social Change*. He retired as Professor of English from the University of Poona.

V M Madge has submitted a doctoral thesis on T.S. Eliot to the University of Poona, and has published poems and articles in journals. He is at present Head of the Department of English at Waghire College, Saswad, Pune.

R S Singh has done his Ph.D. on 'Psychological Schools of Literary Criticism'. Besides more than two dozen articles in different journals, his publications include *The Indian Novel in English*, *Absurd Drama* and (in Hindi) *Matthew Arnold: Alochak*. He has also translated the poems of Donne into Hindi. He is Professor of English at Kurukshetra University, Kurukshetra.

Kalpana Wandrekar worked for her Ph.D. on the theme of displacement and the social-psychological perspective of immigrant characters in Indian English novels. She teaches English at Nowrosjee Wadia College, Pune.

R K Dhawan did his M.Litt. on Comparative Literature and Ph.D. on the fiction of Joseph Conrad. He is the author and editor of several books, particularly on Indian English fiction. He teaches English at Bhagat Singh College, New Delhi.

Ramesh Dnyate obtained a Ph.D. from the University of Poona for his work on the novels of R.K. Narayan. A novelist in Marathi, he is at present Lecturer in English at Ahmednagar College, Ahmednagar.

Makarand R Paranjape is the author of *Mysticism in Indian English Poetry*, and of *The Serene Flame* and *Playing the Dark God* (poems). He has edited *Sarojini Naidu: Poetry and Prose*, *Indian Poetry in English* and *An Anthology of New Indian English Poetry*. A recipient of the Homi Bhabha Fellowship for 1991, he is Reader in the Department of English at the Central University of Hyderabad.

Shirish V. Chindhade wrote his Ph.D. thesis on Contemporary Indian Poetry in English. A regular participant in the Countrywide Classroom programmes on Doordarshan, he is Principal of M. U. College, Pimpri, Pune.

Vasant A Shahane (d. 1988) was the author of fifteen books and about a hundred research papers in different fields of literature. An E.M. Forster scholar, Dr. Shahane turned to the writing of novels after his retirement as Professor of English from Osmania Univesity, Hyderabad, and published *Prajapati* and *Doctor Fauste*. He was a Visiting Professor at the Univesity of New Hampshire, USA, when he passed away.

Vrinda Nabar teaches in the Department of English at the University of Bombay. Her doctoral thesis was on 'The Making of the Indo-English Poet'. Her critical work has appeared in academic journals in India and abroad. She was the editor of the 'Fiction of the Month' page in *The Independent*, and frequently appears in television programmes on books and writers.

O P Mathur is the author of *The Closet Drama of the Romantic Revival* and of several research papers in Indian and foreign journals and anthologies. He retired as Professor and Head of the Department of English from the Banaras Hindu University,

Varanasi. He is at present Vice-Chairman of the Indian Association for English Studies, and Principal Investigator in a UGC project on Major Indian Literature.

Viney Kirpal is the author of *The Third World Novel of Expatriation* and has edited *The New Indian Novel in English: A Study of the 1980s* and *The Girl Child in 20th century Indian Literature*. She has contributed articles to several anthologies and international journals. She is Professor of English and Head of the Department of Humanities and Social Sciences at the Indian Institute of Technology, Powai, Bombay.

Nissim Ezekiel is a well-known poet, and author of several volumes of verse and prose. He has published plays, edited several journals with distinction, and written on topics of cultural and social relevance. A winner of the Sahitya Akademi award in 1983 and the Padma Shri in 1987, he retired as Professor of Literature from the University of Bombay.

Introduction

I

At the UGC Seminar on the Image of India in the Indian Novel in English, held at the University of Poona in March 1986, Professor Nissim Ezekiel, who was one of the distinguished participants, raised his hand after virtually every paper to ask a fundamental question: was the novel on which the paper was based a good novel. The question irritated quite a few people present in the auditorium. What was the point of asking such a question, they felt. If an experienced academic had chosen to write a paper on a novel by an established writer who was very much a part of the literary canon, then the assumption, naturally, was that the novel was good, and no further attempts to show *how* this was so, or *why*, were required. The paper reader, then, was absolved from such a responsibility, and was free to discuss the content of the novel to his heart's content, in keeping with the general theme of the seminar.

And yet Professor Ezekiel, as a poet and critic, was putting his finger on a genuine dilemma that teachers of literature face all over the world. Is it possible to give equal weightage to content and form in the classroom and elsewhere? It is so much easier, and perhaps so much more natural, to talk about the *ideas* expressed in a novel or any piece of creative literature, rather than its craft, that the latter is often conveniently glossed over in academic analyses. Seminars like the Poona seminar only make matters more difficult, because (as in this case) the very nomenclature indicates a privileging of content over form, leading to interpretations of the term 'image' as idea or concept, rather than as simile and metaphor.

The seminar was meant to trace the development of the Indian novel in English during the twenty-five years between 1960 and 1985. Why was the year 1960 chosen as the starting point, and not 1947 or 1950 which historically would seem more significant? Surely, there are some very important novels that such a demarcation automatically excludes: Mulk Raj Anand's *Untouchable* (1935); Raja Rao's *Kanthapura* (1938); G.V. Desani's *All about H. Hatterr* (1948); Bhabani Bhattacharya's *He Who Rides a Tiger* (1952); and Khushwant Singh's *Train to Pakistan* (1956). These novels are regarded as milestones in the history of Indian writing in English. However, it was felt that it was only in the 1960s that the sensibility of the Indian writer in English crystallized into what may be called a post-Independence sensibility, marked by an expression of the private voice. As Meenakshi Mukherjee explains, the fiction of this period "has turned introspective and the individual's quest for a personal meaning in life has become a theme of urgent interest for the Indo-Anglian (*sic*) writer."[1] Interestingly, the 1980s, which set off the upper limit of the proceedings, witnessed a further intensification of the private voice in a bid to liberalize and liberate it from the shackles of social responsibility. Viney Kirpal, one of the contributors to the present volume, says in her book *The New Indian Novel in English: A Study of the 1980s:* "Although the marking of periods is an arbitrary exercise, both the 1960s and the 1980s Indian novel are different because they reflect a recognisable change in the national sensibility, expression and literary form. Both periods are characterized by tremendous literary creativity and it is worthwhile to take a brief look at other aspects of experience such as the economic, political and intellectual trends in India during these years to identify the ways in which the times may have produced the particular sensibility that gave rise to the creative outburst in the 1960s and the 1980s."[2]

Both Mukherjee and Kirpal thus pave the way for an identification of periods or phases in post-Independence Indian English writing, four decades of which are already over. Most scholarly works still tend to lump the entire body of post-Independence writing together, while in reality it should be thought of at least in terms of its early and later phases, each reflecting a unique kind of development.

A more complex issue is that of canons. How is the Indian English literary canon formed? Moreover, in academic enterprises such as conferences and seminars, should only writers of canonical status be included in the deliberations? Naturally, it is far more difficult to objectively formulate a foolproof canon when we are dealing with our own contemporary living authors, than with others. Literary politics play an important role in the shaping of a canon, and only the naive would overlook this fact. But once these dangers are accounted for, and precautions taken, it is possible to arrive at a working definition of the Indian English canon, which may tentatively be said to be made up of writers who have at least one substantial novel published by a reputed trade publisher at home or abroad, and which potentially may be included in university syllabi anywhere in the country; a novel, in other words, which is first widely read by society as a whole, and is then taken up selectively by the academic community. In the final analysis, of course, it is only a writer who consistently writes and publishes, and whose every novel fulfils the criteria outlined above, who can hope to have a definitive place in the canon. Almost all the writers represented in the present volume are established canonical writers in that sense. And yet there are difficulties. Can a Rama Mehta, with only one well-known novel to her credit, be strictly regarded as 'part of the canon? At the time of the seminar, Salman Rushdie had published only two major, controversial novels and was living in England. Was he already a part of the Indian English canon? The case of Shouri Daniels is less ambiguous, because by any criterion that one may employ, she falls outside the canon. However, by one of those perpetual and continuing ironies that govern our lives, the paper on her novel *A City of Children* happens to be by a writer who is very much within the canon – Nissim Ezekiel.

There is a close connection between the concept of a literary canon and a literary tradition. Not every Indian writer who writes in English may become a part of the canon, but s/he would automatically be a part of the Indian literary tradition. What that tradition is, and whether there is a different one for literature written in the regional languages and that written in English, is a debate that has been going on endlessly. Once again, we may humbly propose that all Indian literature should be regarded as part of single tradition, because the cultural milieu in which it is created is the same throughout the country, although the subculture and the language are different in different regions.

However, an important distinction needs to be made between literature produced during colonial times and that produced in the post-colonial period. There are those who argue that both these types of literature are similar, and must therefore be placed under the same umbrella. But it is an acknowledged fact in contemporary critical discourse that post-colonical writing is one stage ahead in a nation's cultural evolution; while colonial literature tends to be Romantic and imitative, post-colonial literature is Modernist and adaptive. This process cannot be reversed without falsifying history, and a nation's political independence from colonial rule must rightly provide the terms of reference for a critical examination of all its modern literature. In other words, in a colonial context the term 'modern' is closely tied up with the exit of colonial powers from a nation, and its attaining of freedom. This is true not just of India, but of countries with a shared colonial history such as those in Africa and the West Indies.

Once we agree that a real divide exists between colonial and post-colonial writing, and that modern Indian literature in all languages (including English) must be attempted to be seen as part of a great Indian tradition that comprises both pre- and post-Independence streams, the validity of Indian writing in English no longer needs to be questioned, as surprisingly, it is still sometimes done; the self-assured quality of the writing is evidence in itself, enough to render the issue redundant. Perhaps it was alright to ask whether Indians should write in English at a time when the writing was still self-conscious and unsure. But today, anyone who purports to be apologetic about Indian writing in English does so at his own peril. Upamanyu Chatterjee, a distinguished spokesman of the modern breed of writers who emerged in the 80s, says in a recent interview in *The Times of India* that "the new generation of Indian writers in English...wield the language with greater skill and less self-consciously than the Mulk Raj Anand generation did."[3] This skill, this lack of self-consciousness also goes a long way in placing Indian writing in English on a par with that in the regional languages, and strengthens the case for regarding them both as part of the same tradition.

We have so far been talking of Indian English literature in general terms, without accounting for specific developments in each genre. Since Independence, the novel and poetry have developed more rapidly than the short story and drama. The reasons for this may be partly commercial: novels, and of late poetry, have a wider readership and are thus taken up by publishers with greater eagerness than other forms of writing. In the UK and the US literary agents are ordinarily willing to extend their services to writers only if the manuscript in question is a novel. A collection of short stories finds very little favour with them, especially if the writer is unknown, and it is his/her first collection. Drama is an altogether different cup of tea. Publishers as a rule usually only print plays which have been professionally performed all over the country. In India, with Indian English drama being confined to amateur theatre productions, there is supposed to be, apart from this hitch, the problem of speech. Indians are said to be poor in creating dialogue in English, because English is not a "living language" in this country. In an article entitled 'Wanted: A Good Indian Writer in English', Rajeev Patke says, "It is not surprising... that Indian drama in English is virtually non-existent. How shall a dramatist arise and do justice to the language of a community so stilted and impoverished except as in parodic reflection?"[4] Reputed publishing firms like OUP and Seagull Books of Calcutta perpetuate such a bias by including in their lists only plays originally written in Indian languages like Bengali, Marathi and Kannada and later translated into English.

Poetry, which was until recently thought to be an esoteric art, has suddenly made great strides with the appearance of prestigious publishing imprints in India such as Rupa, Disha Books and even Viking Penguin, which have turned out new titles with great regularity. In the last decade of the 20th century, poetry seems to be outdoing the novel, judging by the number of young men and women who are taking to the writing and publishing of verse. As Makarand Paranjape says, "If the 1980s were the decade of the Indian novel in English, the 1990s are surely the decade of Indian poetry in English."[5]

II

The novels in the present volume have been discussed chronologically, according to their year of publication. We feel that such an arrangement will help readers to respond to the changing face of India better. The first essay, by Professor K. R. Shirwadkar, looks at Raja Rao's 1960 novel, *The Serpent and the Rope*, from a Marxist point of view, and finds it unsatisfactory for its Brahminical chauvinism. However, the global failure of Communism in our own day is almost anticipated by Raja Rao (in Orwellian fashion) in *Com-*

rade Kirillov which he published in 1976. Although Dr. Makarand Paranjape's paper on the latter novel is thus an answer to Professor Shirwadkar, he is catholic enough to conclude that "India is not a culture and civilization which is primarily spiritual (as Raja Rao implies in the novel) but rather a plural space open to various contesting world-views and ideologies."

The way in which old institutions disappear, or give way to new ones, is surely an indicator of the growth and development of a nation. Manohar Malgonkar's *The Princes* (1963) deals with the now defunct institution of royalty in India, and attempts to trace its decline. Ten years earlier, Mulk Raj Anand had also written a novel on the same subject, which he called *The Private Life of an Indian Prince* (1953). It is significant that after Anand and Malgonkar, no Indian novelist has tackled the subject in a major way; it is something we clearly seem to have left behind us.

Professor R.S. Singh's paper on Kamala Markandaya's *Possession* (1963) brings us back to the realm of spirituality. Perhaps, in the light of India's changing economic character, with market forces being allowed to take control, his thesis that Indian spirituality is superior to Western materialism needs to be reviewed and reexamined. Moreover, it is doubtful whether the novelist herself intends to view the problem in terms of such binary opposites. In our opinion, *Possession* is a complex novel in which the author intends to expose the Swamy as much as she does Caroline, for ultimately the motives of the Swamy in reclaiming Valmiki are as suspect. However, Professor Singh takes a more balanced approach towards the end of his paper when he suggests that ultimately it is a blending of Eastern and Western values (as typified by the character of Anusuya) that seems to be the desired aim of the novel. In the fifties, this was envisaged as the future of free India. The architect of such a forward-looking approach was, of course, Pandit Jawaharlal Nehru, who hoped that while India retained its ancient values, it would also imbibe and assimilate those qualities of the West that would put it on the path of progress and modernity.

Like *Possession*, in Anita Desai's *Bye Bye Blackbird* too we have a fine example of the 'East-West' novel. *Bye Bye Blackbird* appeared in 1971; by the end of that decade, 'East-West' novels had become something of a thing of the past. However, *Bye Bye Blackbird*, like most of Anita Desai's other fiction, is also a trendsetter of sorts, in that for the first time in Indian English writing we are offered a complex, sophisticated analysis of character, in this case the emigrant, in terms of psychological states like schizophrenia. In all her novels Desai uses psychology as the dominant discipline in the shaping of character; this, together with the formal handling of various literary devices, and the attention that she pays to craftsmanship, puts her on a plane quite different from any other Indo-English novelist before her. She is our first 'modern' novelist in some sense, and is immensely fascinating to critics. In the present volume, this is reflected in the fact that she is the only writer who merits as many as four essays on her work.

Professor Vasant Shahane's article on *Fire on the Mountain* (1977) looks at the novel mainly for its form, and concentrates on the sources of its imagery and the use of Time. Similarly, Professor Vrinda Nabar writing on *Clear Light of Day* (1980) discusses the use of Time in the novel as what she calls the "fourth dimension" of reality. Professor Nabar also shows us how Anita Desai, unlike her senior contemporaries, is able to portray the new urban-educated middle-class Indian with great understanding: it is a segment of society to which she herself belongs, and which she knows best. Yet, in the importance that it places on family life and the 'virtue' of chastity, *Clear Light of Day* is as 'Indian' as any novel can be.

Professor Viney Kirpal's piece on *In Custody* (1984) is once again a close reading of character as depicted in that novel. Professor Kirpal also discusses the setting of *In Custody*, an aspect that is often overlooked. As a nondescript Indian town, complete with its dirt, debris and communal strife, Mirpore is perhaps a more real place on the map of modern India than Malgudi. It aptly fits Nirad Chaudhuri's description of small towns. He says: "In India country towns are much worse than big cities – they have all the squalor of their overgrown relatives, but none of the amenities."[6] However, as Professor Kirpal points out, *In Custody* ends on a note of hope and optimism that belies the image of India as dead and stagnant.

The influence of Anita Desai on younger writers is strong. Since she appeared on the literary scene, the sensibility of the Indian writer seems to have undergone a transformation, become modernized as it were. The late Arun Joshi, who despite a small output managed to attain a permanent place in Indian English fiction, was an outstanding heir to Anita Desai's legacy. *The Apprentice* (1974),

Joshi's third novel, deals with an aspect in the ever-changing fortunes of India, which is quite typically a post-Independence phenomenon – corruption in public life, based on a sudden realization of the importance of money. Partly set in Delhi, the novel almost finds its objective correlative in another Delhi novel, *A City of Children*, published in 1985. *A City of Children* is Shouri Daniels' pejorative description of Delhi; while Ratan Rathor, the protagonist of *The Apprentice*, obtains the job of a clerk in this 'city of opportunities', the characters in *A City of Children*, set in a women's college, are academics, domestic servants, peons and chowkidars. While the former novel deals broadly with the theme of corruption in public life, the latter traverses the more private terrain of sexual infidelities and illicit relationships. Both novels, however, are a testament of the process of modernization, with all its attendant ills.

In R.K. Narayan's *The Painter of Signs* (1976) and in Rama Mehta's *Inside the Haveli* (1977), a premium is placed on orthodox moral values, especially in matters relating to the man-woman relationship. Insofar as these novels imply that human beings, and more so women, can only find happiness if they strictly adhere to Indian traditions, and shun everything 'perverse' that is imported from the West, they represent a somewhat dated point of view. However, one cannot afford to miss the irony in *Inside the Haveli*, and conclude, as Dr. Shirish Chindhade does, that the main objective of the novel is to stress the importance of *dharma*. To us, *Inside the Haveli* is also a novel of liberation.

The arch-novel of liberation is, of course, Rushdie's *Midnight's Children*, a major turning point in the history of Indian English literature. *Midnight's Children*, in several ways, represents a forward thrust in India's cultural evolution. 'Displacement' and 'rootlessness' are no longer words to be ashamed of; rather they are taken for granted, and even viewed mock-ironically and mock-humorously by the protagonist, Saleem Sinai; and in this and other ways, an older modernism in replaced by a more meaningful post-modernism. As a child of post-Independence India (even his physical features closely resemble India's), Saleem Sinai is a pluralist with many, fragmented identities, unlike his earlier counterparts in fiction who were more unified and integrated. Besides, as Professor O.P. Mathur so ably points out in his paper, *Midnight's Children* is a truly post-colonial novel in the way in which it confronts head on not the imperial

British powers, but the Indian government (of Mrs. Indira Gandhi). Rushdie is thus a spokesman of a society come of age. After *Midnight's Children*, the Indian English novel was never to be the same again, and even the most outstanding names in fiction from the Indian subcontinent – Amitav Ghosh, Vikram Seth, I. Allan Sealy, Shashi Tharoor – cannot help but being compared to Rushdie, who becomes their role-model.

III

The editors are thankful to all the contributors for their prompt response. We are grateful to Mr. Kamalakar Bhat for his editorial assistance and to Ms. Sunita Nagpal for typing the manuscript.

Department of English, *Sudhakar Pandey*
University of Poona *R. Raj Rao*

NOTES

1. Meenakshi Mukherjee, *The Twice-Born Fiction: Themes and Techniques of the Indian Novel in English* (New Delhi: Heinemann Educational Books, 1971), p. 204.

2. Viney Kirpal (ed.), *The New Indian Novel in English: A Study of the 1980s* (New Delhi: Allied Publishers, 1990), p. xix.

3. 'On the Road', Interview with Sagarika Ghose in *The Times of India Sunday Review*, 22 November 1992, p. 6.

4. Rajeev Patke, 'Wanted: A good Indian Writer in English', *New Quest*, 59, Sept.-Oct. 1986, pp. 313-320.

5. Quoted by Mohan Ramanan in *Indian Review of Books*, Vol. 2, No. 1, October 1992, p. 29.

6. Nirad C. Chaudhuri, *A Passage to England* (New Delhi: Orient Paperbacks, n.d.), p. 47.

K R SHIRWADKAR

Literature as ideology : Raja Rao's *The Serpent and the Rope*

Social movements in India in the nineteenth and the early twentieth centuries were influenced by two opposite tendencies. One was the liberal ideology strengthened by modern education, endeavouring to eliminate the influence of traditions over Indian life and looking to the West for social and cultural ideals. Raja Rammohan Roy was the pioneer of this movement which was taken up later by M.G. Ranade, G.K. Gokhale, S.N. Banerjee, Jyotiba Phule and other leaders, and also by the Brahmo Samaj and the Prarthana Samaj which looked forward to a radical transformation of the social structure in India. But soon the movement met with strong opposition from the conservatives who feared that social radicalism may end in a loss of national identity. B.G. Tilak, Aurobindo and others were the representatives of this counter movement. The tension on account of the two opposite ideologies left its mark on contemporary literature. *The Serpent and the Rope*,[1] written in 1960, is a rather belated reassertion of the Hindu view of life, though its belatedness could be explained by the fact that the novel endeavoured to transmit the Indian world view to the West. Ramaswamy's father advised him that "India should be made more real to the West," and this advice indicates the motivation to write the novel. It appears to coincide with the efforts of intellectuals whose principal preoccupation was to rehabilitate the Indians' pride in their past, in their heritage and in themselves. It was inevitable that the reassertion took the form of aggression, and confidence was manifested as egotism.

In *The Serpent and the Rope*, Raja Rao tries to define the concept of Indian identity and the novel becomes a spiritual history of the hero-narrator Ramaswamy. The concept of identity is based on the traditional notion of Brahminism courageously confronting the greater challenges of science, communism and psycho-analysis from all over the world.

Ramaswamy, the hero of the novel, is a complex and confused man. Though there is a streak of egotism in all that he does, or rather in all that he says, he, a holy vagabond, uprooted from the material reality, appears to be unhappy and his goals in life are uncertain.

There is some sort of psychological problem in his life, of which he is not fully aware but which is the source of his actions and reactions and even of his ideas and visions. He admits that he disliked his father and loved his mother intensely. In addition, he had an abnormal obsession for his sister Saroja. He was unmoved when his first son, Pierre, died, for he tells us that he did not love him. The Oedipus and Orestes complexes have dried the springs of his life and made him humourless and resigned. He is described as a prince and a demi-god by his family and friends but his career appears to be unimpressive in all respects. He suffers from an agonizing sense of loneliness. "Left to myself," he says, "I became alone and full of love" (p.11). He is alone, but affections are not bestowed on him. It is not impossible that his quest for the lost mother led him to the quest for the motherland — India. He says:

> I was born an orphan, and have remained one. I have wandered the world and have sobbed in hotel rooms and in trains, have looked at the cold mountains and sobbed, for I had no mother. (p.7)

The problem of determining the extent to which the metaphysics of self-identity is a conscious device to clothe an inner discord at the unconscious level owing to the loss of his mother, is one which Ramaswamy would not be interested in solving. It is difficult to discuss whether the image of Mother India is a surrogate for his mother because Raja Rao, who had identified himself with his hero, in a defensive strategy, expressed his disbelief in the competence of psychoanalysis to explore the human mind. Ramaswamy says:

> Psycho-analysis, after all, is only like the Indian magician who

can make the mango grow before you, but cannot eat it. (p.106)

He believes that the problem is not for the psycho-analyst to explain, but for the metaphysician to name, and thus blocks at the very beginning any possibility of exploring the dark corridors of his mind. Ramaswamy is conscious of his Brahminical superiority and that too of the southern variety. He says at one point:

> The fact that I was a Brahmin by birth and South Indian seemed to have given me a natural superiority. (p.33)

Madeleine finds a Brahminical 'aura' around him. The novel begins with his assertion "I was born a Brahmin, that is, devoted to Truth..." (p.7), and he is proud of his *gotra*, his genealogy traceable to the great scholar Yagnyawalkya. According to him, the Brahmin has the distinction of not being a contemporary — he goes backwards and forwards in time, and so has a sage to begin the genealogical tree, and a guru to end the cycle of birth and death. Brahminism thus described ultimately becomes a matter of birth and genealogical heritage rather than of devotion to knowledge. When the Vedantin cannot ignore genealogical considerations, other less learned members of the family naturally take up very conventional positions. For Little Mother it is *something* to be born a Brahmin. But at the same time she feels that northerners haven't the sensibility of living such as the southerners have. Savithri, a northerner, confesses that the northerners are new to civilization, and hence are not as classical in their taste as the southerners. Savithri's mother, whose values according to Savithri are more right than her own, would consider the presence of a Brahmin as holy. Subramanya, Saroja's husband, does not have a high social standing and his family culture does not show refinement; whereas Saroja's family can trace its ancestors to Yagnyawalkya and consider that by Saroja's marriage they are related to "low untouchables". Thus, Ramaswamy and his relatives are keenly conscious of caste and regional superiority. In Ramaswamy, who strongly affirms *Advaita* philosophy, these parochial considerations should be embarrassing. But the Hindu view of life, which on the one hand advocates non-duality between the real and the unreal and challenges material existence, while rigorously maintaining class and caste distinctions on the other, was never perturbed by these contradictions; neither was Ramaswamy or Raja Rao.

The assertion of Hindu identity, the truth and validity of the Upanishadic view of life and the superiority of 'abhuman' civilization are the three major strands confusedly woven together in the texture of the novel which gleams and glitters with brilliant aphorisms and gnomic utterances. The novel projects a glorious image of India which was often either ridiculed or pitied in the West. Raja Rao's India is not the India of poverty and disease, of unbearable heat, dust and drought. It is not the India of Mulk Raj Anand or of Satyajit Ray. In order to create an impressive and radiant image of India, Raja Rao had to ignore the hard realities of life — a great risk to be taken by a novelist — and resort to its strong points — its remarkable achievement in the world of metaphysics and mystic philosophy, its meaningful myths, rituals and its spiritual heritage.

Ramaswamy endeavours to establish an Indian identity partly because his father had said that India should be made more real to the world and partly because he was brought up in the Upanishadic traditions right from his childhood. It is not so much Indian history or Indian geography that attracts him; India as a metaphysical entity enthrals him and makes him sentimental. He firmly believes that India is beyond history because it has a permanence which no event can disturb and no revolution can destroy. India lives by inner prosperity and this inner direction of her living offers to her people an emancipation through the knowledge of the self. India is a continuity not in time but in space. She is more of an idea than a reality — hence she is within us and is everywhere. India is Truth, she is the guru of the world. The memory of India sends Ramaswamy into ecstasy: "It is beautiful and sacred to live and be an Indian in India" (p.306). As a sentiment the vision of India with her pristine glory appears to be satisfactory, even exciting, but when it comes to transmuting this vision into details of art or dramatizing it into an image, the writer faces a problem. A few passages, a few characters in the novel might be absorbing; but on the whole, there is nothing that really crystallizes the abstract vision into a concrete and convincing image. Unfortunately, the character of Ramaswamy is full of contradictions, egotism and eccentricities, and is therefore unimpressive. Raja Rao could not do what Saratchandra did when he wanted to transmute the grandeur and nobility of Hindu traditional culture through the men and women he portrayed in his novels.

Another concern of the novelist is to trace Ramaswamy's quest for self-knowledge which, as a matter of fact, could be done only through the travails of life and the rudeness of facts. But Raja Rao rejects actuality and believes only in metaphysical reality. As a result, the myriad problems related to the material aspects of life in this world have no meaning for him. The entire gamut of diverse experiences and feelings which moves the creative imagination to a sense of comedy or tragedy or satire is rejected. The novel attempts to narrate Ramaswamy's determined quest for wholeness, for self-recognition through the path of reason. But some of the fundamental truths of life are taken as axiomatic and are not felt through experience as one would expect in a work of literature. Self-recognition, wholeness of experience, non-duality of life are some of the premises with which the novel starts. These are put to the test only in theoretical discussions marked by a feeble opposition, and are not illustrated or demonstrated by the shared or felt experience of human beings. The novel thus begins where it should have ended.

The novel covers a large intellectual spectrum by way of discussion. The philosophy of the Upanishads, East-West confrontation, Communism, Nazism, Socialism, Buddhism, Catharism, God, good, evil, Marx, Gandhi, Nehru, Lenin, Trotsky, Stalin, Hitler, the man-woman relationship, love, sex and civilization are among the countless topics that are discussed. Ramaswamy receives an assured prominence in all these discussions and enjoys the position of a swami surrounded by well-to-do ladies who listen to him in rapt attention and consider him the final authority on spiritual matters. Even though the range of topics that interests the characters is large, it is not large enough to inlcude the more pressing problems of modern society — poverty, class conflict, caste exploitation, corruption among those in power, and the immoral conduct of the custodians of religion. These problems would naturally be excluded because they are rooted in practical reality which is deemed an illusion.

Ramaswamy's world view is the Vedantin's view of life and from it follows his important comment on two types of civilization. From these seminal ideas a number of consequential ideas emerge which complete his vision. He, a true Vedantin, questions objective reality which turns out to be illusory. What is true is self-consciousness, the 'I'ness and the 'is'ness; hence the importance of self-recognition (because it is the self which connects the inquiring intelligence with universal consciousness). Freedom is to be found in realizing this ultimate truth or the Absolute, though in actual practice he is very likely to be guided or misguided by illusion (the Serpent). In the darkness of ignorance (lack of self-knowledge) a rope may look like a serpent but that is a distortion which is rectified when the guru brings the lantern of knowledge and shows that what appeared to be a serpent was in reality only a rope. Once the unreality of the material world is accepted history and progress lose their meaning. Any attachment to objects amounts to pursuing an illusion. It is a mistake. It is necessary to have a detached attitude to life as advocated in the *Gita*. Sentimentality and compassion, but not love (and we do not know why not) are rooted in attachment and hence lead us to the world of illusion which has no permanence. They are, as it were, fleeting shadows of the Absolute which alone is true. In a seminal passage Ramaswamy says:

> There can be only two attitudes to life. Either you believe the world exists — and so you. Or believe that you exist — and so the world. There is no compromise possible. And the history of philosophy... is nothing but a search for a clue to this problem: "If I am real then the world is me". It also means you are not what you think and feel you are, that is a person. But if the world is real, then you are real in terms of objects, and that is a tenable position. The first is the Vedantin's position — the second is the Marxist's — and they are irreconcilable. (p.337)

Thus all religions or all ideologies which aim at improving human destiny are trying to reshape or restructure illusions, fearing or trying to contain the "serpent" which was, in fact, only the "rope." All religions and socio-political ideologies committed to the welfare of man are comparable to running after a mirage. In another important passage Ramaswamy says that there are two types of civilizations, the anthropocentric and the abhuman... the anthropocentric civilization, whether it is Purist or Protestant, must be self-destructive. The abhuman civilizations — the Greece of Socrates, the India of the Upanishads and of Sankara, Catholicism (and not Christianity), Stalinism (and not Leninism, Trotskyism) had permanence, because they were concurrent with the law.

All efforts to save man from his predicament are self-destructive because there is, strictly speaking, no predicament as such. Buddhism, Christianity or even Marxism are ultimately poetic because they are concerned with material reality, the practical life of man that presumes duality. Man is isolated and his being a social animal is illusory and therefore has no validity. It is tautology. Certain important conclusions follow from the idealistic position taken by Ramaswamy. History, in the usual sense of the word, is meaningless and Rama affirms that India which is the cradle of non-duality, the highest wisdom, has no history. Progress is obviously meaningless. The impersonal and the objective alone has permanence and will alone be able to build a new civilization because

> The new civilization has to be a technocratic one. It will have to banish the personal, the romantic, the poetic from life... The Perfect civilization then, is where the world is not... (p.339)

Ramaswamy is decisively opposed to anthropocentric civilization which he thinks is self-destructive. The Hindu view of life is abhuman and so is Stalinism, but not Leninism or Trotskyism. Stalin must kill Trotsky for Stalin was the impersonal principle in history and Trotsky was a poetic hero. Personalism, as that of Lenin or Trotsky, has no place in building a civilization.

Grounded in Hindu tradition, Ramaswamy fails to see or has no desire to see that the huge automation of the abhuman or the technocratic civilization has to be repressive as it was in Greece and India. Greek civilization thrived on the basis of the system of slavery and Hindu society on the basis of caste, the upper classes in the social structure maintaining their "permanence" as well as their high status by the exploitation and repression of the wretched and the damned. The centres of these civilizations were at the top, in the upper classes, that doubted in philosophy the very existence of that on which they were happily perched and which they thoroughly enjoyed in practice. Ramaswamy's view reflects the same spiritual elitism, reacting sharply against mass-based civilization. It is therefore necessary for him to avoid speaking about the suffering of the lower castes and the untouchables. If Vedanta has no direct relevance to these problems, India has, and the Hindu view of life has. When Madeleine, in sheer annoyance at Rama's tiring glorification of India, refers to the miseries of Indian women and the so-called lower castes, Rama feels a new bitterness, but does not bother to reply. When Saroja fulminates against the state of women in India, particularly among the Brahmins, Rama characteristically says, "There was no answer to give."

The mechanical philosophy of abhuman civilization, which puts the centre of the life-cycle outside the practical world and activities of man, comes very near the Hindu philosophy of *Karma* which ultimately became a subtle device for erecting a facade behind which exploitation could be safely carried on. These views protected the interests of the upper classes and propagated the elite voice which conditioned millions of people to the view that material reality is unreal and therefore not worth changing and that the predicament of the present is a result of one's past. Very naturally, a reactionary political ideology flows from these anti-human views. "If I were not a royalist," says Ramaswamy, "I would have been a Communist." Being emotive in nature this amazing remark need not be critically examined for its queerness. Communism, however, is decidedly anthropocentric whereas monarchism is not; and communism believes that man is a social animal whereas the Vedantin does not lay emphasis on his being social. What is striking is Ramaswamy's championship of monarchy, a discarded institution in modern times. Kingship based on dynastic hegemony is for Ramaswamy the ideal of human civilization. The view that 'the king can do no wrong' becomes justifiable because king is impersonality incarnate. Even holiness of art (Shakespeare) is said to be due to the happiness of King or Queen (Elizabeth).

The *Advaita* view, totally severed from materialism and life and its sufferings, inviting compassion and angry protests, thus becomes monstrous (Stalin had to kill Trotsky) and mechanical. The abhuman has to become inhuman. The non-duality view inevitably runs into a strong reactionary trend because the upper class has to give a philosophical or metaphysical justification to maintain its stranglehold by championing a mechanical, ruthless, efficient social structure, and once stabilized, the hierarchy must not be challenged. The will to change therefore was against the fundamental divine law and so was the action flowing from it.

The cat-kitten philosophy which is the core of Raja Rao's next novel, *The Cat and Shakespeare* is another manifestation of the same view. The abhuman centre of human history had the same passive impact on man. His destiny was not considered to be the central concern of human praxis. Though in metaphysical discussion the guru is entrusted with the task of showing that what appeared to be a serpent was only a rope, in actual life the social hypnotists have loudly proclaimed that it was only a rope when it was really a serpent and people have perished. Another consequence of the *guruwad* was to delegate or subjugate oneself to an external authority and forfeit claim to any independent thinking or voice of dissent. All these elements, built into the framework of the Hindu view of life, gave an unusual stability to the hegemonic structure of society. Hindu hegemony, that is, hegemony of the upper classes in Hindu society, found the philosophy of non-duality convenient to maintain the status and the domination of the Brahmin. The world view expressed by Ramaswamy has all the reactionary elements in it. It is the world view of the upper class.

Ramaswamy naturally does not believe in history or progress which according to Marx is man's effort to emancipate himself. The *Advaita* philosophy advocated by Ramaswamy is averse to social change or social transformation, whereas the Marxist ideology believes in dynamism and transferability of the human world. *Advaita* philosophy considers reality to be stasis. Beneficiaries naturally consider the *Advaita* view as convenient because it rejects change; for change is unreal, and so is progress and so is history.

Ramaswamy finds it difficult to bring together the three tenets of his faith which are (i) his identity as a Brahmin (ii) his love for India as an embodiment of Truth and (iii) *Advaita* philosophy which questions and rejects the reality of material objects. These tenets are inspired by different factors but their motivations are ultimately rooted in the world view of the middle class. Behind the facade of containing Western-oriented liberalism and trying to reassert its own status conferred by tradition, this world view tried to foster its newly gained position. When times began to change and the hegemony of the middle class was confronted by the revolt of the common man, the middle class brought forth the shining shield of the Indian past or the Hindu view of life.

What is wrong with the novel is wrong at the very core; its rejection of worldly reality for the ultimate reality, of the infinite variety and splendour of the many-coloured dome of this life for the white radiance of the Absolute, frozen and freezing, and giving no life-blood to the organic structure of the work. There are many characters in the novel, but, with the exception of one, none reveals the competence of the writer in the art of characterization. It is only Madeleine who, in spite of her early renunciation, is beautifully human; so too, to some extent, is Little Mother who smiled when she got her long-lost *idli* on her northern journey. Otherwise it is a cold world where men, women and children die without bringing about sorrow and suffering in others and people talk philosophy without understanding its responsibility. It is the world view of the writer that devitalizes the novel from the beginning, a world view which is fascinating in the rarefied realm of metaphysics but is of dubious value in a work of art.

Ron Shepherd has pointed out inconsistencies in Ramaswamy's different statements. Though Ramaswamy claims to be objective in his thinking he becomes extremely subjective in his approach to historical fact. As Shepherd says:

> My point is that these inconsistencies reflect the paradox inherent in the stance of the conservative rebel. [2]

But there is hardly any serious motive in Ramaswamy to reform his ideology in accordance with changing times and there is hardly any sense of rebellion.

Ramaswamy shows no effort to live with the times and justfies his refusal to change by refusing the very idea of change. His high subjectivism leads him to the recognition of self but the self does not lead him to the self of others, to the wider reality and predicament of suffering humanity. Like some of Narayan's heroes, Raja Rao's hero can spiritualize his self but cannot socialize it. He is therefore driven to live and brood in the lonely towers of his mind. "I am, therefore the world is. I am, therefore Savithri is." This sophistry leads him to Laxmis and Savithris and finally to a guru and the story of the sage ends here, leaving the reality behind. Ramaswamy makes a significant remark at the end of the novel, a remark which explains his tragedy, the tragedy of the author of *The Serpent and the Rope* and the tragedy of his caste:

> Had I been less a Brahmin I might have known more

"love". (p.407)

What is true of love is true of life. The novel, with all its undeniable grandeur, remains, on account of its uninspiring and uncreative world vision, a splendid ruin.

NOTES

1. Raja Rao, *The Serpent and the Rope* (London: John Murray, 1960), p.11. All subsequent references are to this edition.

2. Ron Shepherd, 'The Conservative Rebel: A Type of Indian Hero', in *Perspectives on Raja Rao*, ed. K.K. Sharma (Ghaziabad: Vimal Prakashan, 1980), p.176.

V M MADGE

Rise of the demos: A study of Malgonkar's *The Princes*

*And what rough beast, its hour come round at last,
Slouches towards Bethlehem to be born?*
— Yeats, *The Second Coming*

The birth and rise of this 'rough beast' is one of the chief concerns of Malgonkar's novels, at least up to *A Bend in the Ganges*. It is in *The Princes*,[1] however, that this theme stands out most prominently, as the novel deals with the decline and fall of princely India. When we take into account the difficulties involved in winning sympathy for a member of the erstwhile ruling classes of India, we begin to marvel at the success of Malgonkar. An enquiry, therefore, into the means with which he accomplishes this Herculean task would be instructive. One of the aims of this paper is to argue that, if *The Princes* is symptomatic of Malgaonkar's novelistic art, one fails to understand the paucity of critical attention he has so far received. A writer who can write such a novel deserves to be hailed as a major figure in Indo-English fiction.

In the first place, the contrast presented in *The Princes* is not a naive one between a glorious princely past and a sordid democratic present. Abhayraj, the narrator-hero, acts as an ironic spectator and commentator on the princes and their India. When his father, the Maharaja of Begwad, says, "... there will always be a Begwad and a Bedar ruling it, so long as the sun and the moon go round," Abhayraj finds this claim slightly comic in the face of British paramountcy on the one hand, and the rising tide of self-rule, nationalism and democracy on the other. Similarly, he mocks at the fantastic idea of the "third force" evolved by the Chamber of the Princes. Abhayraj is the only one who does not enjoy a false sense of security at Lord Wavell's assurance to the princes. He is the only one who recognizes the stark fact of their imminent doom, who sees the writing on the wall, as it were. Moreover, he is fully aware of the human tendency to romanticize the past and dwell over it nostalgically. He says that he knows

> most of the people would gladly give up their right to vote for a return... to the good old days of the Maharajas, the rough and ready justice on the spot, the large number of holidays, the pomp and pageantry, freedom to drink, dance and not have to pay income tax. They cannot divorce the creeping joylessness of life from the change in administration. (p.63)

After Independence, people recall the days of Abhay's father and say, "in the days of Hiroji Maharaj, we used to get wheat at sixteen seers to a rupee.... He was a real food-giver, the *ann-data* was our Dada Maharaj" (p.7).

Abhayraj dismisses all this as sentimental nonsense and calls it a tragedy of those people ruled "by instinct more than reason, sentiment more than logic." He is honest enough to admit that "the old order had little to do with the cheapness of food and clothing" (p.64).

It is this ironic detachment that lends credence to the narrator's description of the princes and their 'socialistic' successors. It is, again, this ironic detachment in presentation that never allows the characterization in the novel to become simplistic. Such awareness of the complexity of human character marks Malgonkar's difference from and superiority to a novelist like Anand. Anand's characters are usually drawn by referring to their social class. All the underdogs are necessarily angels and all the brahmins and maharajas necessarily devils. Malgonkar's characterization is definitely an improvement over Anand's; the difference between the two is the difference between a novelist who uses the fictional medium as a means of propaganda and one who is primarily interested in the act of story-telling in and for itself.

It is interesting to note the changing attitude of Abhayraj towards his father. At first he finds him a slightly comic figure, but he ends up identifying himself with the values heroically cherished by the maharaja. The maharaja of Begwad appears assured in his strict observance of the meaningless durbar etiquette and formalities. He appears heartless to Abhayraj in his treatment of the maharani. It is only Abhay's own involvement with Minnie at Simla, that removes the "barbs of intolerance" in him. Again, he is prevented from making a laughing-stock of himself in the Minnie affair, as much by his own war-experience as by the protective shadow of his father hovering over him wherever he goes. After his return from the war, Abhay is mature enough to assess his father's character more objectively. He notices his father's daredevilry. He always goes after the wounded tiger alone, the most dangerous act a man can undertake. His knowledge of the jungle merits comparison with that of the best hunters of the world like Jim Corbett. In fact I have a suspicion that Malgonkar has Corbett in mind when he describes the maharaja's jungle lore:

> And if he went after the wounded tigers, you did not feel that he was flaunting his courage; he was that rare combination, both the marksman and the shikari,... he could tell by the track of a snake whether it was poisonous or harmless, could call up a tiger by answering its roars, making them a challenge or a mating call... He could read a game-trail better than his most experienced shikaris; a blood-drop, a bent leaf, the droppings of animals, a blade of grass springing back into shape were like sign posts to him. (p.305)

If one reads Jim Corbett's *Jungle lore* or *Man-eaters of Kumaon*, one will find a close similarity between Corbett and the maharaja of Begwad as shikaris.

It is this daredevilry that enables the maharaja to face unarmed an angry mob of five thousand demonstrators and win them over to his side by the sheer force of his personality. The police, as usual, appear only after everything is over. Such an act of heroism is possible only when a man feels that he is monarch of all he surveys. Abhay does not forget to mention the maharaja's weak points, especially his dislike of "that man Gandhi and the white-cap-wallahs".

Because Malgonkar shows the weaknesses of the representatives of democracy he has been accused of injustice in drawing their characters. And yet a figure like Lala Vishnu Sharan Das in *Distant*

Drum is no doubt one of the 'local Gandhis' who sprung up and have been proliferating with incredible speed since Independence. His "Now the party and the gourmet are the same," is a statement characteristic of the uneducated local leadership throughout the country.

In *The Princes* Kanakchand represents the upstart demagogue. He is an 'untouchable' boy and was Abhay's school-mate. Abhay mentions his good qualities — his honesty in returning the *Highroads Treasury* to Abhay, his anxiety for Abhay's health when he suffers from food poisoning and his general intelligence, which Abhay admits, was higher than that of some other boys from upper-class families. So to begin with, Kanakchand was "sound as a silver rupee". It was politics that turned his head and made him lose certain human qualities like gratitude. He carries with him till the end the humiliation of being horse-whipped by the maharaja, conveniently forgetting that the punishment was for cheating examiners in the essay competition. He also forgets that the royal family financed his higher education. He avenges himself on the royal family for the ills done to him by the iniquitous, age-old caste system. From the speech he makes after he becomes the Education Minister, it can be seen that he is more happy at the fall of the royal family than at that of the British Raj. He walks out of the negotiations with the dewan when the Begwad State proposes to hold general elections. All this shows that Kanakchand's envy has made him take up the camouflage of moral idealism, so typical of our socialist leaders. One remembers here Bertrand Russell's pertinent comment, in his essay, "Envy", that envy is the source of much moral and political idealism.

Apart from this complexity of human behaviour, I find the use of the word 'Prince' in the novel significant. The word refers not only to the social class of a person but also to certain human attributes. There are at least three occasions on which the word is used in this way.

The first occasion is when Abhay takes Minnie out to dinner in Simla. In fact, Minnie is the first girl Abhay has ever taken out. He compliments her on the perfume she is wearing. Minnie replies that she had to empty her bottle of Chanel Number Five. Abhay reassures her that he will buy her some more. Minnie says, rather blandly, that she does not know how he can ever get that perfume since there are no imports. Abhay, like Prufrock, does not dare to make a pass at Minnie, as he is under the romantic illusion of Minnie being Punch's 'girl'. His constant reference to Punch puts Minnie off. When Abhay admits that it is the first time he has taken a girl out, Minnie reminds him that he might have gone away without saying goodbye to her. Abhay says that he does not know how to get in touch with her. Minnie laughs amusedly at this simplicity of heart and says

> It's just as well you are a prince. Otherwise you might have found life much more complicated. (p.141)

The second occasion is when Abhay goes through Tony Sykes' 'effects' after the death of the adjutant. He finds Minnie's letter to Tony in his wallet. Abhay knows that Tony was his rival in winning Minnie's favour. In his simplicity he had imagined that Tony could not go far in giving presents to Minnie, and that, pitted against a prince, Tony, the adjutant, was sure to lose the battle. Abhay had casually given Minnie a pearl necklace. Tony had had to borrow money from a Marwari in order to give silk stockings to Minnie. From Minnie's letter Abhay comes to know his place in her affections. He then admires Tony's reticence about his relationship with Minnie. The rivalry over Minnie had never interfered with Tony's feelings for Abhay. He was a perfect lover and a perfect friend. And here was Abhay, mean enough to taint his friendship with the thought of Minnie.

> And yet I was aware that Tony did not lack resources, for he was a man complete in himself, he was the prince, not I. (p.209)

This time the word 'prince' means manliness and magnanimity of heart, as evinced by Tony Sykes.

The third occasion is when the maharaja gives champagne to everyone at Abhay's house in Delhi. The maharaja is extremely happy with Lord Wavell's assurance to the princes that the British government would honour the constitutional guarantee given to the princes by Queen Victoria. This creates a feeling of euphoria in the Chamber of Princes. In his celebration on the occasion, the maharaja, like a true prince, gives champagne not only to Abhay and his wife but even to the domestic staff. This all-inclusive humanity is in keeping with the tradition of basic aristocratic generosity.

Thus the word 'prince' acquires a connotation far beyond its usual class denotation. One of the themes of the novel is to suggest that the qualities associated with princes — simplicity of heart, magnanimity and aristocratic generosity — have disappeared with the passing away of that order. Some incidents in the novel bring out the contrast between these royal qualities and a more democratic state of affairs. For example, there is the meeting between the maharaja and the government secretary, the meeting between the old princely ruler and the new bureaucratic ruler. The meeting is held in an office in shabby surroundings. The building is ugly, dilapidated files are stocked indiscriminately and the office stinks of urine. And on top of all this is the pettifogging bureaucrat. Anyone acquainted with government offices will readily see that the picture has not changed much even today. The meeting starts late, the secretary makes the maharaja wait outside the office out of sheer spite and also because he is busy eating oily samosas and tea. The maharaja, annoyed, goes away leaving everything to the good, old, faithful dewan and Abhay. When they are at last allowed inside, they find, to their disgust, the empty cups and dishes lying on the table. The petty bureaucrat has not cared to present a clean, decent profile.

During the meeting, the bureaucrat shows some more unpleasant aspects of a personality typical of his species. He puts his finger sometimes on the letter of the law and sometimes on the spirit, as it suits him. The meeting is an excellent encounter between the debonair, tactful, statesman-like dewan and the mean, petty bureaucrat. The difference between the two can be seen in the fact that the dewan is well-versed in the Indian tradition and knows the pulse of the people, while the bureaucrat is utterly insensitive to their feelings. When the question of the dam comes up, the bureaucrat insists that the whole area be evacuated, hardly caring to reflect as to where the local inhabitants, the Bhils, will go and find shelter. The dewan explains his difficulties. There are the family gods of the maharaja, and the state. When the bureaucrat insists that their family gods will have to go, the dewan replies, "You can remove kings, you cannot shift Gods" (p.296).

Besides, there are two other eternal features of the new Indian rulers — corruption and hypocrisy. The 'percentage theory' becomes rampant as soon as the bureaucrats get the power to assess and classify the princes' jewellery. Abhay has the same experience when he starts the dairy farm. The instinct to grab everything, to destroy the princes at any cost is seen in the secretary's insistence on the maharani's personal necklace being an item of the state. Similarly, Kanakchand, who says he is a follower of the abstemious Gandhi, is found drunk when Abhay visits him. Kanakchand has a swig in private in the evening, although he champions prohibition in public.

With such a state of affairs, *The Princes* finally gives the impression best described in the words of Yeats:

> Things fall apart, the centre cannot hold;
> Mere anarchy is loosed upon the world.

In its tragic appeal, *The Princes* merits comparison with Achebe's *Things Fall Apart*. And the comparison is not a fortuitous one. Like Okonkwo, the maharaja seeks a heroic death rather than be ruled by mediocre people. Okonkwo hangs himself when he finds that his people, the lions of Africa, have become sheep, the sheep of Jesus Christ and the missionaries. The maharaja prefers being mauled by a ferocious tiger to being harassed constantly by mean-minded politicians. His manner of death illustrates one of the maxims of Confucius: "Politicians are more terrible, than man-eating tigers." Finally, Abhayraj abdicates his title and rights as a prince in the face of the rise to power of mediocrity.

> We were the princes, no one mourned our passing. We were a jest of history. (p.11)

This is not just self-pity, but a stark historical fact. In the general burst of communal riots after Independence, nobody heard the whimper with which the princes' world ended.

Princely India in the novel is described with such fidelity that a reviewer in *The Times Literary Supplement* commented, "Mr. Malgonkar was either a prince himself and a very royal one at that, or must be the ghost of one".[2] Actually he is neither! His only association with the princes was through his grandfather, who was the dewan of Indore State.

V.S. Naipaul called *The Princes* an "honest" book and yet condemned it as an "exercise in heroic conservatism".[3] He wanted Malgonkar to speak of "those three-legged dogs, those red-coated railway porters swearing and carrying heavy bags on their heads" because that is the India that he knows. I do not know how far one can dictate to a writer what he should write about in his work. One may as well demand that Naipaul should not speak about the house of Mr. Biswas but of whirlwind batsmen like Clive Lloyd and Vivian Richards, and fast bowlers like Marshall and Holding, because that is the West Indies we know. Malgonkar himself has something meaningful to say about this:

> The social life of millions of Indians centres around the dustbins of great cities. Granted. But mine does not; and for me to write about it would be as insincere as a white man writing about a Negro-riot.[4]

Secondly, there is a more general question. It is whether certain areas of experience alone constitute 'life'. No novel can be dismissed off-hand simply because it reflects the social life of a minority, howsoever microscopic. This is a point that needs to be stressed with special emphasis in India.

Finally, no assessment of an Indo-English novel can be complete without paying attention to the way the writer handles the English language. In this respect also, it is remarkable that the *TLS* singled out Malgonkar's use of English for praise: "the measured, stately prose of old England proves itself to be still a serviceable medium."[5] In fact this can be said of all the novels of Malgonkar. His English is chaste and in the old tradition. The 'Indian sensibility' wallahs need not carp at this. They have only to examine the scene concerning Tony Sykes and Jemadar Dongre to realize how deftly Malgonkar can make use of vernacular words in English. His English does not lose its racy flavour; nor does it become unintelligible. In fact, in his use of the vernacular, I again find Malgonkar superior to Anand. The strategy of translating verbatim swear-words from one's own mother-tongue is not likely to succeed in a multilingual society such as ours, for such words, even in English translation, puzzle not only the '*phorener*' but also the 'native'. Malgonkar's place is with writers like Desani or Salman Rushdie who use English with zest and gusto.

K.R. Srinivasa Iyengar, in his pioneering book[6] on the Indian contribution to English literature, has installed Anand, Raja Rao and R.K. Narayan as the Holy Trinity of Indo-Anglian fiction. If one looks dispassionately at Malgonkar's achievement as a novelist, one is convinced that he has altered our perception of the pattern of the past. Yet, it is sad to note that he has not received as much attention by the critics as he should have. It is surprising that C.D. Narasimhaiah's *The Swan and the Eagle*[7] makes no mention of him. Nor does the anthology of critical essays on Indian writing in English edited by M.K. Naik and S.K. Desai[8] give much attention to him. Meenakshi Mukherjee's well-known *The Twice-Born Fiction*[9] also deals with Malgonkar in a perfunctory manner. There appears to be almost a conspiracy of silence among Indian critics over Malgonkar's achievement as a novelist.

NOTES

1. Manohar Malgonkar, *The Princes* (New Delhi: Orient Paperbacks, 1970). All subsequent references are to this edition. (The book was first published in 1963.)

2. *The Times Literary Supplement* as quoted by G.S. Amur in *Manohar Malgonkar* (New Delhi: Arnold-Heinemann, 1973), p.105.

3. V.S. Naipaul: *An Area of Darkness* (Harmondsworth: Penguin Books, 1968), pp.62-67.

4. As quoted by G.S. Amur, in *Manohar Malgonkar*, p.116.

5. *The Times Literary Supplement*, as quoted on the blurb of *The Princes*.

6. K.R. Srinivasa Iyengar, *Indian Writing in English* (Bombay: Asia Publishing House, 1962, 1973).

7. C.D. Narasimhaiah, *The Swan and the Eagle* (Simla: Indian Institute of Advanced Study, 1969).

8. M.K. Naik and S.K. Desai (eds), *Essays on Indian Writing in English* (Dharwar: Karnatak University, 1972).

9. Meenakshi Mukherjee, *The Twice-Born Fiction* (New Delhi: Arnold-Heinemann, 1971).

R S SINGH

West meets East: A study of Kamala Markandaya's *Possession*

When asked by Syed Amanuddin if she was an expatriate, Kamala Markandaya (born 1924) wrote in reply:

> I do not think of myself as an expatriate writer. All my thought processes are Indian, my parentage, religion and schooling are Indian, all my formative factors are Indian.[1]

She maintains that her spirit has not altered, even after years of physical alienation from her people and country. And yet, in her novels she has always evinced full involvement in the conflicts and tensions of those uprooted from the country of birth, and living in an adopted country. *Some Inner Fury* (1955), *Possession* (1963), *The Nowhere Man* (1972) and *Two Virgins* (1973) are obvious examples. Even in other novels where the setting is Indian, the difference between the Indian and the Western modes of life is more than implicit – it causes action. India as a cultural entity is amorphous, diverse and undefined. It is therefore interesting to study how a sensitive author like Markandaya orchestrates her views and, as an expatriate, defines it for her readers. She does not see India as a bolus of an indeterminate glorious past, or as a totally Westernized future. She sees it as a changing reality, ever in flux, with clashes of attitudes, interests and emotions of living contemporaries, and yet maintaining its essential self. She does this with perfect ease and adroitness for the simple reason that she writes about herself, every time with a new set of characters, a different setting and a fresh emphasis. My attempt here is to examine her fourth novel *Possession*[2] to show how she reveals the unstated presence of that essential India which has resisted surrender and yet absorbed quite a lot from foreign cultures.

Possession was published in 1963 as a memoir of Anusuya, a young Tamilian journalist who wrote for newspapers, the BBC and the Bombay film industry. She also wrote novels and published them in London. A lady of contacts and common sense, Anusuya moved between India and England without any problems of adjustment or residence. An *alter ego* of Kamala Markandaya herself, she felt quite at home wherever she stayed — in a London apartment, in a Madras or Bombay hotel, or in a hut in a remote Indian village. She was equally at ease with an ex-prince, a village headman, a glamorous lady or a poor maidservant, a salon or a Swamy. This explains why she wrote with convincing familiarity about racial conflicts, spiritual concerns and social behaviour.

Anusuya met Caroline Bell at a party hosted in a Madras hotel by Jumbo, an ex-prince. A rich, well-born, beautiful divorcee of twenty-eight, Caroline had "spectacular qualities". She was in India in 1949, "like an animal in search of the salt-lick that gives savour to living" (p.3). She needed arrack (the country liquor) and wanted Anusuya's help in procuring it. As Anusuya had written a book on village life, Caroline rightly thought that she could be guided in her venture by her counterpart. It was there in the village about a few hours away from Madras that Caroline Bell met a goatherd, Valmiki, a "strangely endowed" (p.19) boy of fourteen who painted on walls and rocks. He was useless for the family, but was encouraged by the Swamy to paint in the service of God. A social misfit, Valmiki had "brought... nothing but shame and sorrow to his parents" (p.19). Caroline saw the paintings, admired them and decided to take the boy to England to provide him with opportunities and scope for self-expression. Pragmatic and passionate in equal measure, she was also a connoisseur of creative talent. She knew that the boy had the necessary gift, the inner urge to paint, and needed encouragement and a proper environment. The East could produce art but could not commercialize it. She wanted therefore to play the patron and eventually possess the unpossessable. The boy was illiterate and only fourteen, and in England it was compulsory for him to go to school up to the age of sixteen. But she dodged the authorities by wandering about in European countries for two years. This tour and the subsequent one in

America helped the goatherd grow into a sophisticate who could speak English and move with ease among people of culture. Valmiki acquired the desired qualities in stages in the course of six years' tutelage under Caroline till he grew up enough to understand her motives and decide to return to the Swamy back in the village. Caroline gave him everything — encouragement, money and even her body, and yet he could not barter away his freedom for gratitude. She wanted to "own" him and that, he thought, was "not an uncommon inequity" (p.230).

Caroline cannot be charged with cruelty, avarice or meanness, but she cannot be absolved of her crime to "own" Valmiki; to deprive him of his freedom to feel independent and live the way he wished to live. "Like sturdy thorn-trees that seem able to ride the worst storm" (p.21), Valmiki was a man of firm mind and clear understanding. He alone understood the implications of the bargain his greedy father had struck with Caroline:

> Caroline has not bought me. She has only compensated for the loss of a labourer. (p.22)

The Swamy, the surrogate-father of Valmiki, valuing his disciple's freedom to do what he liked, asked him: "Do you want to go still?" and then added, "If you want to, you must" (p.23). The Swamy's voice was steady but "its edges were raw" (p.30) and yet he did not try, even by suggestion, to change the decision of Valmiki to leave him behind, "a lonely figure... on the hillside" (p.30), and desire for himself the pleasures of life. Since it is only through submission to desire that one knows how to master it, the Swamy wisely remarked: "...the sound of chafing... like the croaking of bull-frogs... has little charm" (p.29). Valmiki needed to go through the travails of the flesh to realize that peace with himself was the ultimate aim, and that he had to accept "the sweet as well as the bitter fruits of life" (p.30), to know what life meant. Both in India and in England he tasted love and bitterness and neglect and recognition, and yet finally found that he had no use for money or assurance of social security. Placed in the third cave on a ledge "without precedence," "impersonally," were "a ruby ring, a golden column of sovereigns and a pile of uncashed cheques under a stone weight":

> Promissory symbols all: from the magnificent ring that had never been asked to redeem good-mannered pledges that were empty when Jumbo had given them, to the hoarded coins Valmiki's distraught mother had pathetically imagined would build some improbable bulwark for her son, to Caroline's cheques — new ones all, that she must have sent in frantic chase of him one after the other out of her loneliness; symbols all of powers and influence promising the kind of strength that Valmiki no longer needed, emasculated, meaningless now, and arranged here in dumb show. (p.230)

Valmiki had come to attain that serenity which the Swamy had already achieved. The Swamy had toured the world, lived in luxury hotels and also with his disciples, and yet returned to the same wilderness where he could contemplate on freedom, show compassion to the rejects of society, and live in peace with himself.

Valmiki's own growth as an artist in terms of loss and restoration of his spiritual nature confirms the view that there was no stasis in that wilderness despite apparent stagnation; there was a movement within, a kind of agitation that refused to be limited to the physical and the mundane. What the Swamy cared for and Valmiki realized was that what mattered was the spirit and not the body, the vision and not the vista, the creation and not the clod.[3]

This is the essence of Indian philosophy, which pervades the modern consciousness. Obviously, therefore, the Swamy symbolizes the presence as much as the continuity of the values by which our ancestors lived. Although the same age as Caroline, the Swamy, like Shankaracharya, was *jitendriya*, master of his senses. The choice between Caroline and the Swamy was as hard as the choice between the flesh and the spirit, the illusion and the essence. One has to wade through the flesh to attain a state of beatitude. Valmiki opted for the harder path to be true to himself, for he knew that mere sensuality leads nowhere.

As a goatherd, Valmiki had painted a sprawling vine on the four walls of the house of the headman and various gods of the Hindu pantheon in imitation of what he had seen with his own eyes. The last painting he did before embarking for England was Anusuya's portrait "with lowering brows and brooding eyes and a somber mouth" which showed her "forgetful of self and absorbed in another" (p.41).

Even the full-length nudes of Ellie, the twenty-year old Nazi victim, were painted realistically. And the worst in the series was Caroline's picture, "a nude Caroline lying in pleasurable swoon on a sandy beach in the sun" (p.185). It was sensuous, fleshy and what Caroline wanted to see, but it was not art because, as Anusuya rightly thought, "there was no evidence here of any watchful inner eye" (p.164). Anusuya rightly expected that like any artistic expression, "... the painting must somewhere reflect the painter" and Valmiki was "also capable of the most irrational and the impassioned action" (p.163), but he was not yet through the process of maturation. He proved to be a perceptive painter when he attempted painting after shedding the lopsided values of his adolescence — the period spent in the West, when he was between fourteen and twenty years of age. Anusuya observed:

> Now he seemed to have achieved a middle stage serenity... There was too a change in his work so subtle it might easily have been a flight of fancy: but to me there seemed to be moving extraordinary yearning in the human countenances he had depicted, upturned toward the light, quality of compassion and profundity in the divine images that had never been apparent before. (p.230)

Caroline was unable to accept self-expression as the purpose of art, and therefore was unable to see and appreciate this revelation of the inner self of Valmiki in his later paintings. She saw him only as "a wasted man," wasting his work in the wilderness of India. The Swamy, on the other hand, maintained that there is no waste in the work man does "to glorify his God," and in support of his contention he said:

> There are temples, churches, cathedrals... men have put all they possessed into their building and adornment but the names of the creators are lost — yet even you, lady Caroline would not look on it as squandered labour. (p.231)

Caroline, too alert to be subdued, retorted that Valmiki's work was "buried in a hole in a hill" and had only the Swamy to glory in it. For the Swamy, the joy of creation was enough justification for any creative activity as it manifests "the divine spirit". In Caroline's opinion, the purpose of art was imitation and communication, and it was necessary for it to be shared by an audience. And the larger the audience the better it was for the artist, she maintained. On the contrary, the Swamy believed that creation was its own justification as it was service to God, the Great Creator. In the tradition of Indian art and literature which has celebrated the artist's anonymity as a mark of humility, the Swamy was right to subordinate the transitory and flighty recognition that human audiences accord. The cave paintings of Ajanta, sculptures of Ellora or friezes of innumerable temples are here the obvious references. The basic difference between Caroline's views and those of the Swamy — the Western and the Eastern view of art — is seen here in terms of what it does to the audience or to the artist.

In contrast to Valmiki is another painter in the novel: Annabel, a girl of eighteen, educated in Switzerland, distantly related to Caroline, who enjoyed the "illusory freedom" of "her own charmed conservative circle" (p.199). Using love as the trump card she left her girl friends to set up her home with Valmiki in an Italian room to have her rival Caroline "dispossessed". But when she learnt from Caroline about Ellie's suicide, she rejected Valmiki for his failure to recognize his responsibility to Ellie who carried his seed in her womb. Valmiki, thought Annabel, "ran away" from his commitment to Ellie because he did not "even know what decency means". She disdained his Brahmin sensibility, his escapist "wholly eastern sentiments... about the sanctity of life". She spoke this in vengeance to hurt him and left him gasping for breath before he could snuff her out of his life the way he had snuffed out Ellie and his child.

Daughter of a Regent, Caroline was born in India but was English. She had loved Valmiki and admired his art, and yet she knew that like other foreigners he was "emotional" and "unstable," unlike the British,[4] and therefore was untrustworthy. Annabel too found Valmiki different: "... you aren't like us" (p.207), she said. But this dissimilarity was racial and therefore cultural, and was very different from that which his parents had noted about him for being dreamy unlike other goatherds. Westerners can command ritual answers even in situations of strain but Valmiki could not, as despite his six-year conditioning in the West he acted "in a harsh prohibition that he could not ignore". Anusuya who had travelled around the globe "had a puritan streak" within her which withheld her from accepting the West "as a passionate preference". Despite moving from "acrimony to admiration" for Caroline, "the white Narcissus," she retained her middle-class attitude "to live in defined circumspection". But she knew that to Valmiki and the Swamy, the two "spiritual nomads," circumspection in any sense was unacceptable. Anusuya was not a critic, nor did she demonstrate any special talent — she wrote for various agencies, mostly on a commission basis. And yet she was a writer of some distinction. Caroline, the compulsive promoter of art and literature, had thrown a party to boost the sales of one of Anusuya's novels. Anusuya wrote about India, her homeland, and published in the West for wider circulation, and lived an independent life. But Valmiki, being extremely poor and illiterate, became a total parasite on his patroness, leaving his destiny in her hands by surrendering to her his initiative, his right to self-determination and the choice of his bed partners. He found it easy to follow the courses chartered for him, but he also discovered to his dismay that the Pegasus of his imagination was no more free to fly. Valmiki, like any expatriate, "would have to return to it again and again when that strength was drawn," Anusuya averred, "or his reserves ran low, to recharge himself" because "however western influenced, it was from India that his strength came" (p.170). It becomes evident from this that rootedness is one of the essential conditions of an artist. Cultural differences may cause alienation and anguish but it should be admitted that they add sharpness to sensibility, and provide a distinctive flavour to literature of various locations. Valmiki's genius wilted in the formal dampness of the West. He needed the Indian sun to tend him:

> Yes, he said, gently contemplative. Indian Sun. Dazzling. Blinding. You never get it like that here, do you? Sometimes you burn your hand touching the rock it got so hot. May you think of the terrible power there was up there... you always ended up thinking of god. (p.155).

Valmiki's is a symptomatic case. He went to the West at an impressionable age when women, wealth and glamour all attracted him and deflected him from the path urged by the inner voice. In place of experiencing the joy of creation, he indulged in the pleasures of the senses. This distraction was necessary to know what life means; a tranquillized body does not act as a halter to the free play of imagination. But the sense gratifications were neither of his seeking, nor were they without humiliation. He was to Caroline what his money was to him. He was not accepted as a person; he was recognized only for his talent, which had its fallow periods. He had to depend on freakish inspiration like the first poet Valmiki whose anguished heart had exploded into poetry on seeing the wounded curlew. Valmiki's recognition in the West was in terms of money, but never in terms of humanity, the kind of recognition he got in India from the Swamy. Caroline and the Swamy, the two admirers of Valmiki's art, proved to be adversaries, each exercising power on the other in full knowledge that neither would yield to the other. Caroline felt ill at ease when she was alone or with the Swamy, but the Swamy was always at ease with himself [5] despite "tensions of an intransigent egotism". Caroline had "iron and steel" in her personality, and came of "a creed that never accepted defeat". So the contest of wills, the clash between the Swamy's "absolute assurance" and Caroline's infallible "faith in herself" was meaningful only until Valmiki had formed "the protective shell". Once he had become "fully fledged, able to question the right of the questioner to question him" (p.193), he could make his own choice, rendering their context meaningless. He had returned to the wilderness of the village deliberately, assured that he was "no stranger to the wilderness" and that he did not need the "satisfactions" that she had given him and which he knew she could provide in the future too. He had observed in the past that although the words of encouragement spoken by the Swamy and Caroline were the same, their effects on him were not identical. Encouragement came genuinely from the Swamy — without expectations, without any motive, whereas in the case of Caroline, encouraging words came out loaded with her secret desire to commercialize his skill.

Caroline's acceptance of Valmiki's talent was conditional. She admired the potential painter in him and not the person whose personality was inextricably aligned with the painting. The artist who creates may be different from the person who suffers, in one sense, but the two are not separable from each other like the dance from the dancer. Caroline did not care to respect the unique 'otherness' of Valmiki, the human individuality. In her eagerness to elicit the maximum from her investment in the young painter she lost control over her language and reactions. With food and care she had given him "the decency of a healthy boy" but she was downright offensive when she asserted with emphasis that she had obliged the boy by taking him out of "the crevice of the rocks" and by providing him with the necessary facilities and freedom to work. He resented being compared with a worm, for he was aware, however vaguely, of his worth as an artist:

> Somewhere implanted within him, however deep and dormant was the seed of knowledge of his power, and it gave him the bearing which is also conferred on the truly innocent, the walking saint. It had kept his head high even when he was a discredited goatherd; and it sustained him even now, in full fledged knowledge of the shackling of his strength — a wasteland of the spirit most dreadful to man to inhabit because he cannot compute its terms or be certain of enduring till its end. (p.49)

So his reaction was sharp to Caroline's scornful description:

> No, I not crawl out like lice — she beg me, I come. She not like I go back to Swamy. To Swamy, not hole in stone like belly lizard. You go tell her that! (p.54)

In Anusuya's perception, Valmiki was both an ardent participant in, and an onlooker on his place in the opulent culture of the West, the world of Caroline. She observed: "...there still remained, for good augury, vestiges of a cold and watchful inner eye, as disdainful of others as of himself" (p.110). True, Valmiki was "capable of the most irrational, impassioned actions" (p.163) and had accepted "so many lopsided values" (p.164), but he was "not entirely rapt in fatuity" (p.164). It was not without significance that he had painted Caroline's beautiful and innocent face "as false and as empty as the blue illusion of sky..." (p.185).

Caroline's face was false, devoid of genuineness, and was empty, it reflected nothing. Deep down within herself she was empty; all that she had was the flesh and animal instincts. Her "nymphen needs" far exceeded the limits of decency. Ignoring the difference in age (she was fourteen years older than Valmiki) and the motherly role she had assigned herself, she used him to assuage her desires: to possess him fully she drove Ellie to despair and suicide; and finally she used Annabel to humiliate Valmiki. Although she had decided on impulse to take the young painter to England, and had rushed to Madras to claim him back in return for the satisfactions she had given him, she was spider-like, a perfect schemer. She manipulated the destinies of those who came in contact with her — Valmiki, Ellie and Annabel. One by one, each was made a victim of the traps laid by her. Even Anusuya was commandeered to cooperate with her. Anusuya herself confessed, "... not only Valmiki but I, also, had come within the orbit of her powerful influence" (p.119). Anusuya observed about Caroline's powers:

> Her warm, bubbling, insincere power entrapped you: it forced you to respond, even if you suspected it was part of a training that enabled her to be amiable, and exact amiability, precisely whenever she wanted to. (p.181)

Caroline was Machiavellian in her approach to life. She had an eye for beauty and art. Disagreeing with Anusuya, she maintained that for appreciating art one needed only "half an eye" and not "knowledge". She loved art, so she declared that the headman would be a vandal if he washed down the walls to erase Valmiki's paintings. She saw every painting done by Valmiki and even stayed for two weeks in the village to have more paintings done by him. She showed tremendous patience, and interest in the simpleton. She was called "bizarre" and "evil" and yet she was not a "faint-hearted woman". Her father had been Resident for Jumbo's ex-state, a political adviser, and now Caroline was a cultural adviser to the creative genius of India. It came very naturally to the British to rule:

> She was faring, needless to say, extremely well. Wherever the British go, as the whole of the East knows, they live on the fat of the land, though the British themselves have no inkling of it. Simply by taking it for granted they have the hypnotised natives piling it on to their plates. (p.114)

With "divide and rule" ... a formidable inherited skill (p.226), Caroline too used forgery, deceit and lies to defeat her enemies, ensuring Anusuya's complicity in her stratagems — Anusuya, the intellectual who had learnt assiduously "English pallor, accents, manners and disemphasis" (p.88), which Valmiki was to learn in six years till he became "a finished article" needing no further refinements.

Anusuya formed the bridge between the two worlds making "the Undilute East" comprehensible to the West which was all too ready to embrace "lap-dog fashion" the "soulful East" (p.110). Valmiki's success in England and America itself was a result of the resurgence of interest in Indian art and culture after Independence in 1947. Valmiki, an inhabitant of a remote village, did not have any idea of history, Indian or European. Interest in India and Indian culture and history had come into fashion.

> Being handsome helped Valmiki with Caroline. Being Indian helped him generally and massively, for India had come into fashion. Fashionable to know of India, fashionable to know Indians, fashionable to admire its art, fashionable to welcome its women and even, at a pinch, its men. (p.125)

Valmiki had the talent and the "living English legend" (p.5), Caroline showed "her talent in recognising his talent" (p.125); it was a poignant combination of looks and talent. For recognizing his talent, Valmiki laid his cheek against Caroline's hand "the way a dog will" (p.12). Even when he was dissociating himself from her to stay in the Indian wilderness, he "took her hands in his and kissed them — the wrists, the open palms" (p.230), in acknowledgement of his obligations.

India had its own measure of attractions to offer the West — its creative talent and self-sustaining spiritual strength. Caroline came to the village to discover Valmiki and claim him in the same way as European and American women came to a hotel in Madras to seek "tranquillity" from the Swamy. Unhappy to surrender to their men in the traditional way, those liberated women with "out-thrust bosom and shoulders of an unrelenting aggressiveness" came to conquer India, but ironically enough they found themselves happy "to surrender" to the equipoise of the Swamy. Although they formed only "a morbid section of the West", they represented the common factor of subtle deformity of human civilization; that is, the "pinched, down-drawn mouths of permanent discontent". They had to agree with the Swamy that this world is not "a joyless void". It is one's inner strength that sustains life and not material aids. What gives meaning to life is the faith that "one can never be a misfit in the service of God". Even the deformed ones, who lived around the Swamy, had their place in the world in the same way as Valmiki or Caroline who were also misfits in some way or the other.

This philosophy had distinguished the Orient from the West. But the physical condition of India was appalling in the years following Independence — the period with which the novel deals; that is, the period from 1949 to 1955. With low-door huts, malaria-ridden patients and scraggy bullocks, Valmiki's village looked dreary. But with the resurgence of love for local colour (p.88); folk culture;[6] reformation of land laws, which included Abolition of Inams (p.165); developmental programmes undertaken by the local government, with loans drawn from Russia, America or England (p.171); and the changing attitudes of the Indians to themselves, which implied self-confidence and readiness to stand on an equal footing with the world, the map of the village had been changing fast. Anusuya could see this happening as she visited Valmiki's village thrice before he returned to adopt it for good. It was symptomatic of what was going on in the whole country in the early years of Independence. As a result of this physical transformation and also increasing prestige of India in world politics, the East-West consciousness lost much of its sharpness. The Caroline-Swamy antagonism cannot be so violent today as it was made out to be in the early fifties.

There are certain remarks scattered in the novel that reveal ideas that have formed the bedrock of Indian society and culture and have distinguished the Indian ethos from that of the pragmatic West. These are relevant to an understanding of the image of India, and are as follows:

a. Simplicity fosters honesty but affluence wilts it. The ill-mannered Valmiki was an *enfant terrible* in the beginning. But in course of time, as Anusuya observes, "much of the uncouthness was gone and some of the honesty" (p.109).

b. Deflowering a virgin is unthinkable for a Hindu. However nondescript a Hindu, Valmiki wouldn't have copulated with Ellie, thought Anusuya, had he not known that she had already been ravished by Nazi soldiers (p.114).

c. Theories of health and hygiene abound in India and everyone claims perfect knowledge. The Hindu Hotel's manager in Madras expatiates upon his theory of sleeping on hard beds for proper rest to the spine (p.165).

d. The common man of India has been denied so much over the centuries that he takes life stoically and values contentment as an efficacious philosophy. Ignorant about her rights in the Republic of India, Valmiki's mother accepted everything as God's desire and did not expect the doctor to come to her although patients of malaria could legitimately do so.

e. It is believed that in each human being there is an inner retreat where one can easily repose in moments of strain. Valmiki's mother, even when she was going to die of malaria and consumption, did not show any signs of fear or strain as she was ready to surrender "to the forces that were not so much vindictive as inevitable" (p.175). She had attained serenity, a state of mind difficult to achieve.

f. Incest is viewed unfavourably anywhere, but in India the mother-figure is always sacred and is one of the three mothers that Indians worship, the other two being the cow and the country. Ignoring the fact "that by the criteria of his own country" Caroline was "old enough to be his mother", Valmiki was demonstrably satisfied with his carnal relationship with his patroness, and this had become possible because the last vestiges of peasantry had fallen from him during his sojourn in the West. Had he continued to be a Hindu and not become "a pagan" he would have desisted from the heinous relationship.

g. In India feminine beauty is associated with a fair complexion. Anusuya rightly observed that Caroline was found to be the most fascinating woman at the party given by Jumbo in Madras because "English good looks pass for transcendent loveliness" (p.1).

h. Indian response to modern art is only imitative and derivative so that the Indian reviews of Valmiki's paintings repeated what had been said in Western magazines. Even Anusuya had seen the beauty of Valmiki's paintings through Caroline's eyes initially and through the opinions of the critics of his paintings.

i. Gossiping with the servants is a common pastime with women in India. So Anusuya talks to Mrs. Peabody without any self-consciousness, but this is resented by Caroline.

j. After the merger of princely states with India, princes came to be "two per paise fighting congresswalas for the public posts" as "the power and influence had shifted to the representatives of the people".

k. Remorse and self-condemnation are deemed necessary for the purification of sinning souls. Valmiki indulged in severe self-criticism for snuffing out two lives in ignorance. His repentance is more sincere and severe than "expiation and the easy Christian peace" as Anusuya explains.

Caroline and the Swamy are presented as adversaries, one standing for pragmatism and the other for idealism. Valmiki's choice is between two extremes, which is itself a hangover of that simplistic thinking which sees life in black and white. For those who admire the Buddha and a host of such renunciates of India, Valmiki's decision may seem wise, but it was a decision taken in retaliation and was therefore impulsive. The stridency of the Swamy's tone and Valmiki's temper are understandable, but the sagacity of the decision to stay back in the wilderness remains questionable. Within the novel, therefore, the narrator herself is presented as a foil to Valmiki and as a model of the harmonious blending of Eastern and Western values. In Anusuya's personality there was the happy coexistence of the two points of view — she admired the Swamy as much for his inner strength as Caroline for her manipulative skill and worldliness. She knew that a judicious mix of the two cultures alone could ensure meaningful cooperation in the field of art and literature. This seems to be the logical thrust of *Possession*, which was what was being envisaged in the fifties as the future of Free India.

NOTES

1. Syed Amanuddin, 'Transnational Sensibility: Random Thoughts', *The Journal of Indian Writing in English*, No.2, Vol.13 (July 1985), p.4.

2. Kamala Markandaya, *Possession* (Bombay: Jaico Publishing House, 1967). All subsequent references are to this edition. (The book was first published in 1963.)

3. Dr. S. Radhakrishnan writes: "The distress of Arjuna is the dramatisation of a perpetual recurring predicament. Man on the threshold of life, feels disappointed with the glamour of the world and yet illusions cling to him and he cherishes them. He forgets his divine ancestry and becomes attached to his personality and is agitated by conflicting forces of the world. Before he wakes up to the world of spirit and

accepts the obligations imposed by it he has to fight the enemies of selfishness and stupidity, and overcome the dark ignorance of his self-centered ego. Man cut off from spiritual nature has to be restored to it. It is the evolution of the human soul that is portrayed here. There are no limits of time and space to it." *The Bhagavadgita, with an Introductory Essay* (New Delhi: Blackie and Son India Ltd., 1976), p.95.

4. Even Mrs. Peabody, the maidservant of Caroline who had a lot of sympathy for Valmiki, nursed this view (p.80).

5. The Swamy confessed, "Despite myself I have not been able to forget him (Valmiki) entirely" (p.100). He also understood his human weaknesses: "Everyone makes mistakes...". Addressing himself to Anusuya and also the women devotees in the Madras Hotel he said, "It is you who invaded my solitude, who made me aware of it — made me realise I had sought the contemplating life too soon, that there were lessons yet to be learned in the world... what else should I be doing among you ladies here but sitting at your feet learning my lesson?" (p.101).

6. In the film *Jhansi ki Rani*, which was scripted by Anusuya, the producers used local colour rather liberally (p.18).

KALPANA WANDREKAR

The ailing aliens: Anita Desai's *Bye Bye Blackbird* as a symptomatic study in schizophrenia

Post-Independence India saw the departure of hundreds of emigrants enamoured by the fairyland of orderly abundance in the West. The reasons that prompted this exodus could be many. Emigration could perhaps have been seen as an escape from the communal, economic, and ideological chaos which prevailed in the native land; it could also have been in pursuit of a foreign qualification which would elevate one's position in a society which still looked up with awe and admiration towards the West. Stepping into the much sought-after life in the West, what did the immigrant find? He lost himself in the vastness of cities, tall buildings, the machine-like precision, and the keen consciousness of time. This made him powerless. The sense of independence which he started with was lost.

For an immigrant, confrontation with another society starts the process of destructuring and restructuring the self. He or she is faced with two heterogeneous sensibilities, both of which are conditioned by the intrinsic value systems of their cultures.

The idea of self-chosen identity is essential in a culture whose composition is changed by immigrants, and in which group relations are disrupted by individuals being thrust among strangers. By contrast, as Joanna Kirkpatrick points out, "Identity in a caste society has a fixed sense of social placement."[1] That is why the adaptation expected of Indian immigrants is very hard on the individual. The contrast between the value systems of India and the West is so sharp that the first reaction is that of resistance. This is natural because the communal consciousness which an Indian shares with other members of his society has given him the guarantee of identification and purpose. He is an integral part of the historical past which he has acquired; he is also the living present and he has a definite purpose in contributing to the future. In brief, he has the awareness of the continuity of his own tradition.

Why does an immigrant lack the ability to communicate meaningfully with the alien culture? His identification is restricted, owing to a different orientation. Having been born and having grown up in a particular community, he develops an unquestioning attitude. The responses to the surroundings and to tradition and values are unconditional. He is recognized as a functional part of the common consciousness of that particular community which means that he becomes an integral part of the accepted framework of that society. This establishes a social rapport which solidifies the structuring of his personality.

The encounter with another culture which has developed its inbuilt structures brings the process of individual enhancement to a standstill. The immigrant has to learn it from the outside as he has not grown with it. It demands the cultivation of automatic reflexes which in turn destructures the personality. The adjustment is threefold — social, economic, cultural. This decentralization creates a strain which is likely to erupt in psychic aberration.

This brings us to the contention of this paper that displacement is one of the causes affecting the normalcy of an individual. Schizophrenia can be the ailment of the aliens. In this light, Anita Desai's *Bye Bye Blackbird*[2] is considered here as a symptomatic study in schizophrenia. The analysis is based on the tenets expounded by Erich Fromm in his books, *The Sane Society* and *The Fear of Freedom*.

Characters in Anita Desai's *Bye Bye Blackbird* face the dilemma of finding their identity precisely because their background is rooted in a caste-ridden society with group ascription by birth. From a fixed sense of social placement they are transferred to an alien surrounding where it is an individual who matters, and not a group. Desai tackles this problem repeatedly. Her father was a Bengali and her mother a German. This "has brought two separate strands into my life. My roots are divided because of the Indian soil on which I grew and European culture which I inherited from my mother."[3] This lack of regional identity brings the stance of an observer to her work. In the majority of her works one finds a character trying to adjust, either to the place or the society or to the self. To quote K.R.S. Iyenger, "Her forte is the exploration of a particular kind of modern sensibility that is ill at ease among the barbarians and the philistines, the anarchists and the amoralists."[4]

Anita Desai handles the nuances of the human psyche beautifully. In *Cry the Peacock*, we see how outside pressures drive Maya out of her mind to near-insanity. Nirode's voice in *Voices in the City* echoes the same note of sickness. Characters in *Bye Bye Blackbird* are no exception to this. We find similar symptoms in these characters. Anita Desai herself confesses that their (the immigrants') "schizophrenia amused me while I was with them and continued to tease me when I returned to India... I wrote it in an effort to understand the split psychology, the double loyalties of the immigrants."[5]

In the pattern of arrival and departure of the immigrant characters Anita Desai is concerned not only with space but with the "spatial" (place) effects on the psychology of her characters, for as she comments, "whereas a man is concerned with action, experience and achievement, a woman writer is more concerned with thought, emotion and sensation."[6] All the characters pass through the cycle of attraction, hostility and frustration. In Dev we find the first stage in the evolution of an immigrant character. As Eric Fromm notes, "We are never free from two conflicting... tendencies — from bondage to freedom and another to return to the womb."[7] With this intention to free himself from social and economic bondages, Dev leaves India. He seeks material freedom. To be a student is only a means by which he seeks entry into this material haven. With the entry into the new country begins the process of severance of natural ties. He has to be self-sufficient. The feeling that no one cares is always dormant and with it the nostalgic longing to go back.

He reacts vehemently to the discrimination made at public lavatories and the lambasting in the bus. But, like other immigrants, he is helpless in the environment into which he is thrown. Therefore, his outburst lacks the heartfelt intensity of an outsider. The cynical observer finds himself caught in the cross-fires of a mixed sensibility of love and hate. His response is very quick. At times he is dazzled by the abundance of the supermarkets, at other times he is stung by a word or a phrase directed at him. One thing that is certain is that the slow severance of natural ties prompts him to find others by "relatedness." He compares and relates everything to India. A situation, a scenery brings to his mind either a resemblance or a difference that exists between the two countries. When he promenades down the high streets of London he finds the echoes of a Himalayan mall. It is a great solace to find similitude at least in Nature. This is his attempt to "relate." Still, one hears the resonance of "No, not here, no, not yet" from behind. What hurts him most is the indifference of the people and their pets. He is all the while confronted only with buildings and not human beings. The city has the deserted look of a wasteland:

> If I lived on a road like this in Calcutta, I would be aware — as aware as can be — of everyone around me. But not here. Here everyone is a stranger and lives in hiding. They live silently and invisibly. It could happen nowhere in India. (p.64)

The utter indifference of people makes him feel as insignificant as a particle of dust.

This paralyzes his ability to act, and builds up "the tension in togetherness". Dev comes from a culture which is group-oriented and encounters one which is individual-oriented. At the same time, urbanization in this country has erased an individual's uniqueness. India is backward and preserves an individual's individuality. People from such a background find it difficult to have any meaningful communication with a stereotyped personality of the West who is the very picture of impersonality.[8] Dev is shocked to see the dearth of people in a country where everything is in abundance. He oscillates between certainty and uncertainty continuously like the tick-tock of a pendulum. He finds it hard to seek affirmation. In him, we can say, after R.P. Blackmur, "The expatriate is orthodox as a human type, classic in the nature of his struggle, romantic only in the ordinary sense of being strange in appearance, or nostalgic in some of his attitudes".[9]

Abandoning the idea of further studies, Dev seeks a job frantically but without success. The types of jobs that are available are disheartening, a sort of mockery. His attempt to find a job was the extreme or "historical symptom of the general disorder"[10] in his character. Aptly one can say he was either a waste product thrown off like a rash on the face of the system or he was a serious and significant phenomenon — and the more so when he failed of the disintegration consequent upon the division of function in the social systems of the Western world.[11]

When the attempt to relate fails, insecurity and anxiety result. In the tube, he feels "like Alice falling, falling down the rabbit hole like a Kafka stranger wandering through the dark labyrinth of a prison" (p.66). He had tried to break the bondage — geographical and cultural. But in the process he has not gained freedom but has bargained for another kind of exile. Dev's experience makes him neurotic because he is unable to attach meaning to his experience. He is aware of a state of chaos and confusion in him caused by outside pressure. He realizes that he is losing his balance: "the other part is something he cannot explain, even to himself, for it is only a tumult inside him, a growing bewilderment, a kind of schizophrenia that wakes him by day...". Symptoms of schizophrenia are obvious when Dev falls ill — he is running fever and sees upon the wall "a barrow piled with such fruit as can only be seen in an Indian market" (pp.139–40). Such ruminations definitely reflect the urge to regress to the mother's womb, and more precisely to a known and secure habitat. The severance of natural ties brings into sensitive minds such a disease as schizophrenia. The traumatic conditions explain how difficult it is to break the natural ties. He tries to attach meaning to his life and he is bothered by the question as to why he is here, wasting his father's money. The great turmoil in his mind splits him. It is only at Roscommon James' in Hampshire that Dev finds a romantic healing to his suffering and uncertain wavering. Everything seems to fit into the pattern, and for the first time he feels he is not an intruder, feels acceptance. The whole atmosphere reverberates with Hindu philosophy and religion. He gets a sense of belonging. As Erich Fromm puts it,

> While the infant is rooted in mother, man in his historical infancy remains rooted in nature. Though having emerged from nature, the natural world remains his home, here are still his roots. He tries to find security regressing to and identifying himself with nature. In relating himself to them (parts of

nature) the individual finds his sense of identity and belonging as part of nature.[12]

Dev finds his roots in the landscape at least temporarily. But will it be sufficient to withhold his rejection by society? The answer cannot be an affirmative one. This is because every new experience is frightening, agonizing and revolting — harsh enough to break one's mental equipoise.

If uncertainty is the first stage in the evolution of an immigrant character, incongruity is the second. This is developed in Adit's character. Anita Desai encapsulates the immigrant character when she writes,

> I was fascinated by them. They remained Indian to the tips of their fingers and yet they lived almost wholly English lives... They had turned themselves into brown Englishmen... Yet emotionally they were, if anything more Indian than the Indians at home. Their response to Indian music, food, literature, news and jokes was so enthusiastic as to be a trifle abnormal, pitched too high for comfort. Hardly any of them were able to sever their roots not even those who tried hard. Indeed the roots seemed to have been strengthened by transplantation.[13]

Adit is a prolongation of Dev's character. Trying to accommodate oneself in a new country is like giving birth to a new personality. One has to change, adapt and tolerate. Dev cannot stand the abuses flung at him (like "wog") but Adit is indifferent or at least pretends to be so. He knows he has to live with it. He has made that choice. Like being born, opting to be an immigrant is a negative act. The only difference is that while the former is an accident, the latter is a conscious choice. Though Adit has settled in England for quite some years, he is still a misfit — a fact which he slowly realizes.

> His sleek crumpled face looked incongruous with (completely detached from) this brilliant outfit and was rather like a paper bag mask stuck on top of a gorgeously dressed and opulently stuffed scarecrow. (p.8)

The gown, like society, is an oddity. It is not congenial. The absorption in another culture is impossible not only because people differ in colour but also because the Englishman is conscious of his individual personality whereas the Indian is conscious of his human relationships. Adit's marriage is brought about by such feelings of uncertainty and humiliation. At Christine Longford's cocktail party, the hostess and the guests make him feel humiliated as a result of which Sarah's shyness and rectitude attract him. "Humiliation and uncertainty were not sensations in which Adit felt at home" (p.84), and so he chose Sarah, for something "oriental" in her attracts him — it is an attempt to relate to company.

Adit's marriage to an Englishwoman introduces new conditions of living, weakening the habit of faith and breaking up the settled ways of life. Though he seeks freedom and seems temporarily happy, it appears that this freedom from Indian conventions and poverty creates more problems and grievances, which are sometimes more distressing because they are less familiar. M. E. Derrett observes about Indians:

> Their new self-awareness makes it impossible for Indians to go back, their cherishing of Indianness makes it difficult for them to go ahead.[14]

However happy he may seem, he is treated like an outcast in the flock because the very "species" is different. As Adit is not "familiar" by bonds of blood and soil, he is looked upon with suspicion by Mrs. Miller and the Roscommon James. This rejection, and the realization that his surroundings and adopted culture are bound up with a civilization radically different from his own, result in tremendous frustration. The unsatisfied compulsions of the social and natural environment lead to a regression in Adit's personality. The regression is an outcome of Adit's desire to find unity with his fellow men. His attempt to establish new ties by marrying Sarah fails, and he cannot establish unity either with people or with Nature. The stay at his in-laws' evokes contrasting reactions in Adit's mind. He feels anxious and abstract, but haunted by nostalgia. Everything he sees and hears, he interprets in the Indian context. Gaining freedom has crippled him. He wants to escape from this into a world where he would "pack up all my cares and woe". This is an escape from the fear of the freedom which he had sought, into the tradition from which he had escaped earlier.

The distance in years as well as geography gives Adit a better perception of his country. The Hampshire landscape brings to his mind a revelation of India's "wild, wide grandeur and its loneliness and black, glittering enhancement" (p.207). The shock of his country's poverty and starkness recedes. This is because India guarantees him love, respect, care, security — the very values of life that make living worthwhile.

In Adit's character Anita Desai has depicted that the discovery of the self of an immigrant and the exile he is forced to live in, are parts of a single process. The nostalgia grows with such ferocity that it becomes an illness, an ache. This enhanced susceptibility to illness happens not as a by-product but as a direct outcome of social disorientation. When he returns to his house in Clapham, he is a changed man. He shrinks into isolation and is dumb with despair. He has the painful look of one who suffers — "a look of disbelief that invalids have when the disease is still new, their pains still unaccustomed" (p.206). The mechanisms of escape — to dominate or to submit — do not help him. A sense of being discarded, of not belonging, builds into a crescendo. The footsteps on the pavement sound different; they have, in place of gay briskness, the sound of a shameful escape — escape from enemy territory. He is stripped of the covering of education and his "feel" of British history and literature; the truth that he is an Indian and can never breathe the English air freely dawns on him. He suffocates and is fed up of wearing the label "Indian immigrant". "It's so stifling... being aware of who one is and where one is" (p.216). He cannot bear the sight of another "expressionless British face". He is afraid he might hit him, like Raskolnikov killing the pawnbroker. Now he is ready to surrender his freedom for the sake of being one of the herd. If he doesn't belong anywhere, there is the danger of losing the sense of "I", which preserves sanity. What pinches him most is "not the occasional slights and insults directed against him as a stranger, a non-belonger, that had finally proved too much for him, but the placidity, the munificence and the ease of England" (p.212). He fears a nervous breakdown. At Christine Longford's wedding the symptoms can be clearly seen. He has become nameless. The questions that torment him are "Who am I? Where am I?" He is no longer Mr Sen but a "wog," "Asiatic," or

"Indian immigrant." He gets visions of one who is a psychic case.

> He had a dreadful vision of himself in the white shirt and shuffling slippers of a lunatic's garb at an asylum, an outsider not only by virtue of his colour but an imagination run amuck. (p.219)

This phase of Adit's character reflects suffering similar to what Erich Fromm describes:

> Is it surprising to find in the average adult a deep longing for the security and rootedness which the relationship to his mother once gave him? Is it not to be expected that he cannot give up this intense longing unless he finds other ways of being rooted? In the most extreme form, we find the craving to return to the mother's womb. A person completely obsessed by this desire may be the picture of schizophrenia![15]

The India-Pakistan war is the last straw; it helps to finalize Adit's decision to return to his own clan. This decision reminds one of Sindi Oberoi (*The Foreigner*) who comes to India with the motivation which "meant escape from a bit of myself that appeared the most decayed". Sindi's alienation was of the soul, whereas Adit's was caused mainly by geography.

The cycle is complete and Adit discovers his real self throwing away the garb of a *pukka sahib*. He wants to escape the unreal and artificial life which he is leading in London.

> All our records and lamb curries and sing-songs, it's all so unreal. Whatever it is, it will be Indian, it will be my natural condition, my true circumstance. (p.234)

His nationalism can be explained thus:

> Man freed from the traditional bonds of his native community, afraid of the new freedom which transformed him into an isolated atom escaped into a new idolatry of blood and soil, of which nationalism and racism are the two most evident expressions.[16]

One gets a feeling that if Adit had stayed longer he would have ended up like Srinivas in *The Nowhere Man*.

The different phases in Adit's character are suggestive of the "process of birth". His evolution can be aptly compared to the biblical myth of Paradise.

> Man who lives in the Garden of Eden in complete harmony with nature without awareness of himself begins his history by the first act of freedom, disobedience to command. Concomitantly he becomes aware of himself, of his appearance, of his helplessness, he is expelled from Paradise — two angels with fiery swords prevent his return.[17]

Adit's motherland was his paradise where he lived in harmony with the people of his own soil. When he crosses the threshold of his native land in search of social freedom, he unconsciously disobeys the conventions of his land, with the result that he is made aware of his separation and helplessness. His choice to be an immigrant itself expels him from his native paradise. The "fiery swords" could be interpreted as the acquired habits of material comforts which would, perhaps, not allow him to be at peace with the "backward" conditions in India and drive him back to England. He assures Sarah that if they are unable to live happily then they have the option to go back. As Ortega y Gasset sums up:

> The human organism which seemed an independent unit capable of acting by itself, is placed in its environment like a figure in a tapestry. It is no longer the organism which moves but the environment which is moving through it. Our actions are no more than reactions. There is no freedom, no originality. To live is to adapt oneself, to adapt oneself is to allow the material environment to penetrate into us, to drive us out of ourselves. (*Meditations on Quixote*)[18]

The process of individuation in Sarah is crippling. When she is sent to London for a secretarial course, "the umbilical cord is cut". The severance heightens with her marriage to Adit, and it is complete with her departure from the country.

If Dev fluctuates between uncertainty and certainty, Sarah shuffles between reality and unreality. Her predicament is more intense than that of Adit or Dev because Adit and Dev have the guarantee that they will be accepted where their roots are. But Sarah has no assurance even in her own homeland. She is not very eager to visit her parents. It is duty rather than feeling that makes her meet them. She is constantly and perennially under tension, which makes her life unreal. That is why she is affected by tortures of anxiety and insecurity. The division in herself can be clearly seen in the following monologue:

> In the centre she sat feeling the waves rock her and the fear and questioning began: who is she... Both these creatures were frauds, each had a large shadowed element of charade about it... her face was only a mask, her body only a costume. (p.39)

Her dilemma is that of being uprooted and hence deeper. The harmony of her life is disturbed by her contact with Adit. She is dismissed by her parents and by society and the land she has chosen to live in has no stronger claims on her because of its unknownness. The result is "anonymity". She avoids answering any personal questions and is ashamed of her Indian husband, though very devoted to him. Her self-imposed seclusion is one of the reasons for her anonymity. She confesses to Adit that if he had not married her or if he left her, she would be a lunatic like Miss Moffit. Her introverted and brooding nature fears this outcome and to avoid it, Sarah submits to Adit. Her personality disintegrates. She prefers solitude, a 'moral' solitude which is the result of her suffering. Here the patient feels lost and anonymous. It is the fear of facing the unknown. This psychological frustration leads to a painful outcry:

> If only she were allowed to keep her one role apart from the other, she would not feel so cut and slashed into living bleeding pieces. Apart, apart. That enviable, cool, clear, quiet state of apartness. (p.43)

Sarah is a masochist; it is her way to find unity with the outside world. There are many ways in which union with the outside world can be sought in order to have a sense of belonging. They include masochistic passion (submission) and the sadistic (domineering) one. Sufferers from these try to establish symbiotic relationships. The ultimate result of these passions is defeat.

By submission the person transcends the separateness of her individual existence by becoming a part of somebody. Sarah, when rejected by her parents and society, finds the world around her hostile and tries to submit to Adit — the very cause of her isolation and alienation. She never protests to him and is ever ready to sacrifice anything to save her marriage which is the only way she can transcend her separateness. When Adit explodes, "my son will be born in India" (p.235), she is repelled but still swallows it and submits to the household duties. She refuses a promotion in her job in order to accompany her husband to the East. In fact, the symbiotic nature of the relatedness of Sarah and Adit can be described in Erich Fromm's words:

> Both persons involved have lost their integrity and freedom, they live each other and from each other, satisfying their craving for closeness, yet suffering from the lack of inner strength and self-reliance which would require freedom and independence and furthermore constantly threatened by the conscious and unconscious hostility which is bound to arise from the symbiotic relationship.[19]

Like other characters in the novel, Sarah also yearns for freedom. It is not freedom from conventions or traditions but freedom from the self: the self which carries the stigma of "Mrs. Sen", which she wants to hide, conceal and escape from. It is this self, which after coming into contact with Adit has made people leer at her, and she too has become suspicious of her acceptance anywhere. She wants freedom.

> She could be as eccentric, as individual as she pleased without being noticed by even a mouse. She walked out into the soft muzzling rain with her packages reassured to find herself an unidentifiable, unnoticed and therefore free person again. (p.44)

When she ceases to possess any defined status in society she responds by retreating into exile. Her life too is "silent and empty".

She shuns the world outside because the social value framework begins to disintegrate. "Rain streamed down the window panes she had deliberately left uncurtained for she loved the sight of it closing about her, shrouding her, separating her from the world with its lustrous curtains" (p.45). Her neurosis, like Adit's, is caused by the inability to attach meaning to experience as well as to establish contact with her environment.

With all this, one gets the feeling that hers is the only character which has rich potential for psychological probing but the possibility is not thoroughly exploited by the writer. At the tea party we are told that she is relieved but we are not told about what exactly she feels, the turmoil in her mind. In a play or in a film an actress can show her feelings through expressions but a novelist has to depend on description, on monologue or soliloquy. None of these vehicles is fully exploited to analyze Sarah's character. On another occasion too, when Sarah refuses to play with her childhood toys, we are kept ignorant about the emotions felt by her at that time. Is it that she is reluctant to share her childhood memories with her husband because he is an alien? Or is it the denial of the past? Or again is it the rejection of the association of that English childhood with the present self which is not purely English? The reader simply speculates. The "why" in every case remains unanswered. The writer does not allow us to peep into Sarah's mind. The outer reactions we see, but what goes on within is often known only to the character and its creator.

The novel is neatly divided into three parts like *A Passage to India*: arrival, self-discovery and departure. It makes use of the journey pattern which is in conformity with the unceasing journey of the process of being and becoming. It suggests the flow of life and its permanence. It has two points of concentration (centering around Dev and Adit) and the "split" is "crippling". There is a sudden abrupt change in the focus. The "scene" changes not from one place to the other but from one character to another and in this we have, as Mary Springer describes "the rhetoric of characters in opposition which causes them to reveal each other's values as well as the values in the situations".[20] The portrait of Dev is developed by showing the fluctuations of his mind and the permanence of his identity. On these lines the change in Dev's character is acceptable but the peripeteia in Adit's character is sudden and shocking and therefore unconvincing.

Now the title is relevant in the sense that it is not a mere farewell phrase. At the time of her departure, Sarah is sorry to see that

> It was her English self that was receding and fading and dying, she knew, it was her English self to which she must say good-bye. That was what hurt — not saying good-bye to England because England would remain as it was, only at a greater distance from her. English, she whispered, and then her instinctive reaction was to clutch at something and hold on to what was slipping through her fingers already. (p.255)

The novel concludes with the phrase "Blackbird Bye-Bye" uttered by Dev. Is it that Dev is bidding goodbye to Adit only or is it also to his Indian self?

Dev takes Adit's "place" on both levels — physical and psychological — to continue the same cycle. But as Hari Mohan Prasad comments: "In Anita Desai's novel the acuteness of dilemma is lost in the welter of lyricism and her characters hardly emerge as sharply sketched figures. They are tinsels of loose sentiments or ready-made ideas."[21]

NOTES

1. Joanna Kirkpatrick, 'Women in Indian-English Literature: The Question of Individuation', *Journal of South-Asian Literature*, 12 (Spring-Summer, 1977), p.122.

2. Anita Desai, *Bye Bye Blackbird* (Delhi: Hind Pocket Books, 1971). All subsequent references are to this edition.

3. Ranjana Sen Gupta, 'Sunlight Through Chinks: An Interview with the Novelist', *The Hindu*.

4. Quoted by Shyam M. Asnani, 'Anita Desai: The Novelist With a Unique Personal Vision,' *Contemporary Indian Literature*, XIV, No.1 (Jan-March, 1974), p.6.

5. Anita Desai, 'The Book I Enjoyed Writing Most', *Contemporary Indian Literature*, XIII, 4 (1973), p.24.

6. R.S. Sharma, *Anita Desai* (Delhi: Arnold Heinemann, 1981), p.17.

7. Erich Fromm, *The Sane Society* (London: Routledge and Kegan Paul, 1956), p.27.

8. Manas Mukul Das, 'Modernity in East and West', in *Modernity and Contemporary Literature* (Simla: Indian Institute of Advanced Study, 1968), p.88.

9. R.P. Blackmur, *The Lion and the Honeycomb: Essays in Solicitude and Critique* (London: Methuen and Co., 1956), p.61.

10. Ibid., p.68.

11. Ibid., p.70

12. Erich Fromm, *The Sane Society*, pp.48-49.

13. Anita Desai, 'The Book I Enjoyed Writing Most', pp. 23-24.

14. M.E. Derrett, *The Modern Indian Novel in English: A Comparative Approach* (Beligique Universite Libre of Bruxelles, 1966), p.179.

15. Erich Fromm, *The Sane Society*, p.57

16. Ibid., p.24.

17. Ibid., p.24.

18. Quoted by Krishna Chaitanya, *The Psychology of Freedom* (Bombay: Somaiya Publications, 1976), pp. 87-88.

19. Erich Fromm, *The Sane Society*, p.31.

20. Mary Doyle Springer, *A Rhetoric of Literary Character: Some Women of Henry James* (Chicago: The University of Chicago Press, 1978), p.32.

21. Hari Mohan Prasad, 'Tension in Togetherness: An Explication of Biculturalism in Indo-English Fiction', *Chandrabhaga*, IV, No.4 (Winter, 1980), p.73.

R K DHAWAN

Destiny of a nation: Arun Joshi's *The Apprentice*

Novelists continue to dominate the literary scene in India, as elsewhere. Indo-English novelists until the thirties wrote for a readership largely Indian and unmistakably nationalist. They were so preoccupied with the politics of the day that they had little occasion to turn to 'man'. Post-Independence fiction is free from social and political overtones of a rabidly nationalistic variety. It has concerned itself with exploring the significance of India for mankind, and with the problems that man faces in the twentieth century. The more recent Indo-English fiction has been trying to give expression to the Indian experience of the modern predicament, the fiction of Arun Joshi being the most representative.

A novelist, as artist, aims at creating a new order in his fiction. He is free to promote and project his personal view of the world. He has a right to select, shape and interpret his material. But this cannot be isolated from his historical consciousness which is implicit in this aesthetic conjunction between the self and contemporary history. There is, indeed, a tension between a novelist's right to present his own vision of society and his duty to hold the mirror to Nature, reflecting things as they are. Literature undoubtedly is a reflection of life — a manifestation of human emotions. The novel, because of its particularity in time and space, owes a considerable degree of allegiance to social, political, economic and cultural history. The impact on a writer of the historical milieu in which he lives is of utmost importance. A novel has to be a just and truthful representation not only of human nature, but also of specific circumstances and facts.

No genuine writer can afford to remain contented by being a mere observer of the contemporary situation. Absorption with the issues in one's own time is the primary source of inspiration for a writer. In the contemporary situation, any sensitive writer would find that the odds he has to face are stupendous.

Arun Joshi recognizes a reality beyond the mere phenomenal world, a reality which the artist could imagine and capture by giving a consistent form to the shapeless facts of human existence. The source of most of Joshi's novels is actual experience. Joshi the artist, however, is not content merely to restate experience in a coldly scientific manner. He feels a need to shape it, a need to discover the reality which lies hidden in the actuality of his own life as also in the life around him. A novel, while being a realistic work of fiction, is not a photographic copy of everything that has gone on in society. It is the result of a scrupulous process of selection during which the author assembles all materials from within the social or historical situation, transforming them into a satisfying work of art and giving his own interpretation of the situation, an interpretation which might be quite different from the historian's or the sociologist's.

The fiction of Arun Joshi seems to offer insights into the human condition today. He subjects the contemporary scene to scrutiny and dramatizes his vision of it. Published in 1974, *The Apprentice*,[1] the third of Joshi's novels, is a document of a crucial period of history. It evolves out of a people's historical and cultural experience. In order to evaluate a work of art, we must pay attention to the meaning, the author's intention, the subject matter and the relevance of the work to its immediate community and to humanity as a whole. It is Indian society of the post-Independence era which informs the work. At the very outset of the story, Ratan Rathor, the protagonist, makes a significant remark: "One never knows which is one's last outpost" (p.8). He unfolds the story of his life — his hopes and aspirations, his dreams and fantasies, his agonies and anxieties. The account given by him is not a mere tale of the life of an individual but also the story of a nation's "passage" through a period of trial and tribulation. The destiny of the individual is thus inexplicably linked up with the destiny of the nation in which he lives.

The historical aspect of the novel is quite significant, for it raises a pertinent question about the relevance of history in a work of art. As a matter of fact, historical sense and reality enter into the sphere of art imperceptibly; they are important factors in determining the ultimate value of a given work. In a sense, every novelist tries to enshrine a period in a book. This historical reality, in terms of time and place, forms an integral part of a work of art and is transmuted in the process of giving it creative expression; in the process it achieves wider dimensions of universality and at times a state of timelessness.

The Apprentice is a testimony to the process of moral degeneration that has been taking place in Indian life. It has, as its backdrop, India on the eve of Independence and during the succeeding decades. The novel relates to the time when, enthused with a nationalist zeal, people looked forward to a glorious millennium. But all their hopes were shattered, with degeneration taking place in every walk of life. The novel is concerned with the corruption that power brings with independence. Ratan Rathor's journey of life assumes a representative quality and is at once a record of the hopes and aspirations, conflicts and frustrations, defeats and humiliations of an individual and of a nation.

The Apprentice is not in line with Joshi's earlier novels, for it has a much larger sweep, touching epic dimensions. *The Foreigner* and *The Strange Case of Billy Biswas* record the travails of protagonists who find themselves in the midst of strange and alien circumstances. *The Foreigner* vividly depicts the cultures of Boston and New Delhi; in *The Strange Case*, the scene shifts from New Delhi to the Satpura hills in Madhya Pradesh, the two geographic locations representing two different cultures — the sophisticated and the primitive. *The Apprentice*, on the other hand, does not relate to a particular segment of society but to the whole nation with its moral chaos and gradual degeneration into the quagmire of loss of faith and spiritual bankruptcy. The odyssey of Ratan Rathor is not that of an individual but of the entire nation.

The story of *The Apprentice* is cast in the form of a dramatic monologue. Ratan Rathor is the narrator who "must tell all. All or nothing. What use is a confession if not total" (p.87). He tells his tale to a silent listener — a young student who has come from Punjab to Delhi to rehearse for the N.C.C. parade on Republic Day. Replying to a query about directions to reach the grounds, Ratan finds the young student to be a fit listener to his tale: "Or, if you could wait a little I shall drop you. I go the same way. Can you wait? Good" (p.7). Like Coleridge's Ancient Mariner, Ratan insists that the listener hear him out. Ratan also reminds us of Marlow, the first person narrator in Conrad's *Youth*, who tells the tale of his youth in retrospect to a group of listeners. *The Apprentice*, like *The Strange Case of Billy Biswas*, is rendered in chronological fashion, with sporadic flashbacks interspersing the narrative.

The novel is set in an India familiar to the urban middle-class. Ratan Rathor is both the hero as well as the anti-hero of the novel. Though he does not feel at home in society, he does not abandon it as Billy Biswas had done. Interestingly, he embodies the very world of material values which his predecessors Sindi Oberoi and Billy Biswas had rejected. He is neither a rebel nor a dissident; he is a victim. After feeling alienated from society, he adapts himself to the ways of the world. He has a powerful instinct for survival. He knows that some people survive through defiance while others do so through their abilities. And there are still others who survive by sycophancy and by being servile to those in power. Ratan fully succumbs to worldly pleasures. At every stage he puts up an initial resistance only to discover, like so many of his kind, the futility of his endeavour.

> What was right? What was wrong? No one seemed to know. Or maybe they *knew*, but when it came to practice no one seemed sure whether what was right was practicable. That was where the rub lay. (p.64)

Ratan is a child of double inheritance: the idealism of his father is matched by the pragmatism of his mother. He is greatly inspired by his father's active participation in the country's freedom movement. When he was only ten years old, his father, responding to the call of Mahatma Gandhi, had abandoned his practice as a lawyer and given away most of his wealth to join the revolutionaries. And he had been gunned down by a British Sergeant as he stood at the head of a procession of freedom fighters. The incident, which Ratan had witnessed, made an indelible impression on his mind.

While he studies in college, Ratan is haunted by the memory of his father who had advised him to be good, to be respected and to be of use. He intends to make a mark in life, a mark as visible and striking as his father's. He toys with the idea of following his father and even decides to join the clandestine army of Subhas Bose. His mother, however, vehemently dissuades him from taking such a step. She advises him not to befool himself because "a man without money was a man without worth. Many things were great in life, but the greatest of them all was money" (p.20). She asserts that "money succeeded where all else failed. There were many laws.... but money was law unto itself" (p.20). Margayya, the protagonist in R.K. Narayan's *The Financial Expert*, comes to the same realization: "Money alone is important in this world. Everything else will come to us naturally if we have money in our purse".[2] In both the novels, money strikes the keynote and it is money that introduces the main theme of the book.

Ratan leaves home to seek a career in the metropolis of Delhi, for it "was a city of opportunities. To fail in Delhi would have been the sign of the greatest incompetence" (p.31). Contrary to his expectations, Ratan fails to get help fom his father's friends. Alone, disheartened, deflated, the world appears to him "as a bundle of mirrors, tempting and somehow held together, but on the brink always of falling apart" (p.18). He undergoes a humiliating experience while hunting for a job. Getting a job proves to be by no means an easy task, for no job can be had without manoeuvring. The novelist makes a dig at the way vacancies are filled in offices: "It was expected that the jobs would be filled by people who had, in some manner, been pre-selected" (p.30).

With the help of a roommate at the inn, Ratan ultimately gets a job as a clerk in a government office for war purchases. Although it is a temporary position, he looks forward to a rise: "educated, intelligent, cultured... it was my right that I should rise in life, to levels higher than the others aspired for" (p.32). Henceforth his only aim in life is to make a career.

Quite often Ratan remembers his father's mocking reference to "bourgeois filth", deriding an average man's desire to prosper in life and to make a career (p.33). The wheel comes full circle when Ratan devotes himself whole-heartedly to building his career by means fair or foul. He is in fact shattered by the breakdown of faith:

> What hurts is the collapse of the faith that they destroy. You believe there is justice in the world. You go about the world for fifty years, this belief sitting in your heart. Then something happens and you go seeking justice. And justice is just not there. Or, you assume your wife is faithful, your children love

you, your boss fair, or that God exists. And, then, some day proof comes along that nothing is so. This is what hurts. (p.24)

In order to be confirmed in his job, Ratan has to agree to marry the boss's niece. By now he knows only too well that the world runs on the basis of deals, and

> if men forgot how to make deals the world woud come to a stop... It is not the atom or the sun or God or sex that lies at the heart of the universe: it is deals. (p.51)

Though Ratan progresses in rank, he becomes increasingly fraudulent and unscrupulous: "The more money I accumulated, the more I was dissatisfied and the more I was determined to 'enjoy' life" (p.89). He confesses that he has become a "master faker" (p.28). He has added a new dimension to his life, and he has become, at the age of twenty-one, a hypocrite and a liar. He acquires a sense of docility and obedience. He readily accepts bribes and now owns a car, a flat, a refrigerator and also has twenty thousand rupees in the bank.

At the time of the Indo-China War, Ratan feels strongly for his country which "had come to such a sorry pass" (p.57). He wonders who should be held responsible for the debacle in the war: the ill-equipped army or incompetent politicians. And he comes to conclude that "what was at the root of our downfall was not the military, nor the politicians, nor yet the treacheries of the weather but the Indian Character" (p.57). In his essay on "Crisis of character" Ratan hits out at the corruption in society and describes the Indian people as "a glorious monument in ruin" (p.59).

Ratan doggedly struggles through the political and ethical questions involved when making war purchases until one day he comes into contact with Himmat Singh, popularly known as the Sheikh, and accepts a bribe from him. He becomes completely unscrupulous in the pursuit of his career and ends up by accepting a bribe when he least needs the money. Ratan attributes this to the prevailing degenerated atmosphere. He finds himself trapped in the corrupt system where "men were weighed in Money or Power" (p.65), and he has no other option. He wonders how he can be his own master when a system is his master. He is only a weather-vane or blotting paper.

Ratan derives solace from the evil of corruption which is rampant in society. Justifying his action, he gives us a bird's-eye view of Indian society.

> If I had taken a bribe I belonged rather to the rule than the exception. Peons were frequently taking bribes. So were government officials and traffic policemen and railway conductors. A bribe could get you a bed in a hospital, a place to burn your dead. Doctors had a fee to give false certificates, magistrates for false judgments. For a sum of money politicians changed sides. For a larger sum they declared wars. Bribery was accepted by factory inspectors, bank agents and college professors; by nurses, priests and chartered accountants; by all those who acted in the public interest. Men took the bribes to facilitate the seduction of their wives; women for seduction of other women. All this I knew and had known for twenty years. (p.112)

In Bombay, Ratan signs a deal with the Sheikh and takes a bribe for the supply of substandard war material. He derives satisfaction from the fact that everyone is busy amassing wealth by exploiting the opportunities provided by the war. Some people had started hoarding commodities such as baby food and antibiotics, in which there was bound to be a black market. Even a Member of Parliament, "a trustee of the Republic," feels unconcerned about the war:

> 'Nobody lost a war these days,' the M.P. said. 'There were always compromises. To be candid,' he whispered, *who* cared for the wilderness that we were quarrelling over.' (p.86)

It is the Sheikh perhaps who has penetrated the Indian reality more than anybody else:

> This country had two kinds of people... The rulers and the ruled. The rulers were a fraud... phoney people who knew only how to make speeches, be cruel, and feather their nests... The ruled were brainless. (p.84)

He despises both categories. When Ratan, before entering the deal, shows some reluctance for fear "that people would come to know" (p.75), the Sheikh admonishes him by saying that only fools like him believe that there is a law book laid down by God which they must follow:

> There was no such law book, Rathor, he said. What existed, he said, was not written by God but by a silly society that would do anything for money. (p.76)

The most striking change in Ratan is seen in his sudden interest in wine and women. So far he had lacked the courage to give vent to his desires. But now he ogles at the women around: "I felt bold, unfettered. I stared at them, the women. Openly, wilfully" (p.77). Not only this, he visits prostitutes. In short, Ratan is "at the peak of the dung heap that I had been climbing all my life" (p.85).

The war is allowed to be lost and the Brigadier, upon his return from the battlefront, has a nervous breakdown. The Brigadier had deserted his post during the war, and this desertion was due to the fact that he had been supplied with defective war materials which had been approved of by none other than Ratan. Significantly, during Ratan's boyhood days, the Brigadier, himself a teenager then, had once saved the former's life when he was attacked by a band of hooligans. The Brigadier, yelling and swearing, had leapt across the fallen bicycles to "fight for me, *me*, who no one had ever fought for" (p.17). It is a strange irony of fate that the same Ratan becomes responsible for the Brigadier's death. The situation reminds one of Arthur Miller's *All My Sons* where Joe Keller's supply of defective gas cyclinders leads to the death of his own son, Larry.

Shocked and shaken by this tragedy, Ratan resolves to take revenge on the Sheikh. To his utter disbelief, he learns from him that he alone has not been responsible for the deal: the Secretary and the Minister have also been party to it. Ratan has been made a scapegoat because he is "a spineless flunkey" (p.136). He is merely a tool in the hands of higher-ups. The Sheikh makes a shocking and candid observation of Ratan's character:

> You are bogus, Ratan Rathor, he drawled in a voice that had begun to go out again. Bogus. From top to bottom. Your work, your religion, your friendships, your honour, nothing but a pile of dung. Nothing, he said, but poses, a bundle of

shams.

The Sheikh reveals to him that it is the callous and corrupt society that has made his mother a whore and his sister a vagrant, and that he has been driven to sell his soul to the Devil.

Ratan's morality is so completely eroded that he cannot bring himself to confess his crime to the authorities. He visits the temple to seek peace and courage but he meets a priest who is ready to grease his palm to save the skin of his son, a contractor who is facing punishment for having used substandard material resulting in the collapse of many roofs. He concludes that even religion is not free from corruption and no succour can be drawn from it. The novelist presents an India riddled with corruption. God can be propitiated by gifts in black money to his temples, where the priests themselves are as corrupt as the narrator.

Ratan realizes the futility and hollowness of his whole life. Having lived for two decades, as he says, "in smog: confused, exploited, exploiting, deceiving" (p.138), he is tired in body and spirit. He has neglected India's rich heritage and not created the new order he once envisaged. Penitent, especially after he learns that even the temple priest condones bribery, he takes to cleaning the shoes of the congregation. Each morning before going to work, he goes to the temple and wipes the shoes of the people and then begs forgiveness of "my father, my mother, the Brigadier" and all those he has harmed "with deliberation and with cunning" (pp.148-49). This symbolic act of penance, he thinks, will bring him humility.

Though the future of the country looks grim, the young, as Ratan tells the listener, "might yet hold back the tide" (p.150). The novelist pins his hopes on the new generation and ends the novel on a positive note. There is hope as long as young men are willing to learn and ready to sacrifice, as they have done many a time before. Ratan exhorts the young to rise to the occasion and make a new start. It is never too late.

NOTES

1. Arun Joshi, *The Apprentice* (New Delhi: Orient Paperbacks, 1974). All sub-

sequent references are to this edition.

2. R.K. Narayan, *The Financial Expert* (Mysore: Indian Thought Publications, 1952), p.21.

RAMESH DNYATE

The hothouse cactus: A note on R.K. Narayan's *The Painter of Signs*

Lionel Trilling, in his essay, 'Emma and the Legend of Jane Austen,' has expressed the view that though it is ideal and desirable for a reader to approach a writer without any preconceived notions about the writer and his work, such a thing just does not happen in practice if the writer happens to be a well-established one. He says:

> Every established writer exists in the aura of his legend: the accumulated opinion one cannot help being aware of, the image of his personality that has been derived, correctly or incorrectly, from what he has written.[1]

The observation assumes great relevance as one tries to assess the work of a writer like R.K. Narayan, in whose case, as in Jane Austen's, the legend is 'unusually compelling'. The aura of Narayan's legend presents the novelist with different images: as a conformist in the time-honoured dictums of the Shastras, as a Karma-conscious writer believing in the cycle of *Janmas*, as a humanist accepting the wholeness of life and the pre-ordained scheme of things and, as a comic-ironist watching the absurd drama of human existence with amused detachment.

These 'images' become immensely useful in understanding the novelist's art and his mind, particularly the delineation of his characters. The personal views and convictions of a writer may colour and shape his characters; it is only when they interfere with the lives and sap the growth of these characters, that the reader gets worried and looks askance at the writer.

The present paper tries to argue that the interfering mind of Narayan, the novelist, seems to preclude his men and women from growing, despite the latter's own potentialities. It is here that the man-woman relationship in Narayan's *The Painter of Signs*[2] appears to be an excellent 'case-study' to argue out the thesis. Although other critics of Narayan have touched upon the argument, it is usually put forth either in the form of a generalization or a cursory remark in the context of other aspects of the novelist's art. The exclusive nature of the argument, therefore, may strike a note of difference.

It is interesting to note that even before the publication of *The Painter of Signs* (1976), Narayan expressed his apprehension regarding the reception of his novel. The apprehension of the novelist was born out of the fear that the novel might shock the conventional reader. Says the novelist:

> I think some of my regular readers might be a bit dismayed by some of the biological references, but then you can't very well write about birth control without some mention of sex, can you?[3]

Narayan seems to have taken a narrow view of his readers. He also seems to have overlooked the disquieting nature of his novel, located in the way he himself sealed the fates of the leading pair in it, and not in the "biological references" as he feared.

Narayan has cast *The Painter of Signs* against the backdrop of 1972 India. But even a cursory reading of the novel reveals that beneath the deceptive veneer of modernity the life-cycle of the Malgudians moves steadily, with the same age-old tempo and rhythm. *The Painter of Signs* has a simple plot, narrating the tale of shadow and substance under the guise of a love story, the main players being Raman, the sign painter, and Daisy, the family planning propagator.

Raman, reminiscent of Sriram in *Waiting for the Mahatma*, is realized as a funny kind of "drifting" protagonist. Although he is determined to "establish the age of reason" and talks slightingly of the present-day 'sexplosion', he is, in reality, obsessed with sex. At the beginning of the novel he is caught musing thus:

> He wanted to get away from sex thoughts, minimising

> their importance... but the female figure, water soaked, is enchanting. (p.15)

A little later, at the bangle-seller's shop, Raman observes:

> The bangle-seller... concentrated his attention on a plump wrist — massaging it down to suit the circumference of a bangle. The woman enjoyed it and moaned with delicious pain. (p.21)

A carefree sign painter, Raman, enjoys the company of like-minded friends and the affection of his old aunt. The complacent man accidentally runs into the newly arrived family planning officer, Daisy, and, like his counterpart Raju in *The Guide*, falls head over heels in love with her. He happily agrees to work for her and paint the messages propagating family planning. The enticing company of Daisy, the tough-shelled woman, awakens desire in the bachelor boy and he gets obsessed with a passionate longing to possess her. He accompanies her to neighbouring villages and tries to seduce her. However, she escapes, and he feels dejected.

But Raman, though baffled and humiliated by Daisy, manages to win her over and finally heads progressively towards his cherished goal — the fulfilment of desire. Unfortunately, the Raman-Daisy episode does not conclude in the hero's dream of marriage. Despite his overcoming of Daisy's resistance, the novelist seems to have reserved a pre-ordained lot for him. Just when he is about to taste marital bliss, Daisy, that most enigmatic and tantalising 'mohini', unceremoniously leaves him at the altar.

Daisy is undoubtedly Narayan's most determined, self-made and purposeful woman, perhaps the last word in the women's liberation movement. Running away from a house of suffocating orthodoxy and conventions, Narayan's new woman vows to take up the most hazardous and apparently dull and drab job — the mission of arresting and controlling the country's appalling population growth. Daisy is chiefly realized through the eyes of Raman. She certainly makes an arresting portrayal. At Malgudi, she meets Raman and finds him extremely useful to write, "We Two, Let Ours Be Two" sort of messages. As she is truly wedded to her work, 'falling in love' would never exist in her scheme of things. But despite her cool and grim nature, eventually she too gets involved with Raman.

It may be noted that the first instance of her 'fall' or initiation into the world of the flesh ironically comes after her own thwarting of her seducer's intentions. It is here that Daisy appears to be an improved edition of Rosie. Sensing Raman's obvious desire to be with her, she responds thus: "If you must stay, please bring your bicycle in. I don't want it to be stolen, or worse, seen on my veranda at this hour" (p.113). After the first instance, there follows an uninterrupted routine of togetherness. It continues till she finally leaves Raman for good.

For Raman, Daisy remains a puzzle, an enigma. This most difficult woman revives in him dreams of love when, like an ordinary and average human being, she succumbs to a weak moment. For Raman, life's great ordeal comes to an end when she willy-nilly accepts his marriage proposal, but not before opting for the *gandharva* marriage, and only after he agrees to her fantastic proviso that, "they should have no children... and... if by chance one was born she would give the child away and keep herself free to pursue her soul work" (p.124). Not without reason did Raman jocularly call her Queen Victoria and Rani Jhansi! Daisy, like the goddess-wife in the legend of king Santhanu, threatens to leave him the moment he questioned her or asked 'why' or 'how' after their so-called marriage. But despite Raman's absolute agreement to her proviso, when he eagerly and expectantly goes to her office to invite her as a wife to 'their' house, as was mutually decided, Daisy, without so much as batting an eyelid, gives him an icy and death-like 'No!' Her only excuse is an urgent assignment to arrest the high population rate in a certain region. To his mad, wild and pathetic pleadings, she has simply this to say:

> Married life is not for me. I have thought it over. It frightens me. I am not cut out for the life you imagine. I can't live except alone. It won't work. (p.139)

And Raman, facing the bitter truth that the bride will never come home, muses over his plight in a way in which only a Narayan hero can:

> Raman had a last glimpse of Daisy... He reflected, may be we will live together in our next Janma. At least then she will leave

people alone, I hope. (p.141)

It may be noted that Raman faithfully falls in line with the other Narayan men, like Sriram, Srinivas and Chandran, of the earlier novels. He prefers to live a life of quiet withdrawal and has no other option but to reconcile with his present Karma, as he turns towards the solid and real world of ordinary people.

The ending of the novel disturbs the reader. It is difficult to reconcile oneself to the pre-ordained lot the novelist has in store for Raman and Daisy. If the reader sympathizes with the miserable and frustrated Raman, he is baffled and annoyed by the way Narayan finishes Daisy. It may be noted that her parting company with Raman, as Vimala Rao says, "has not been necessitated — the equilibrium that one has automatically expected is seriously upset..."[4] One is inclined to mention that the 'equilibrium' in the novelistic world of Narayan seems to be upset by the very images of the novelist. It may be worthwhile to consider *The Painter of Signs*, and its ending as factors responsible for the disturbing nature of the novel. One needs to look at the factors from Narayan's point of view, to understand the book's disquieting nature.

Narayan has time and again opted for distilled sex in his novels, and preferred to take a moralist's outlook in the portrayal of sex between his characters. Consequently, he keeps sex at the barest minimum. And when one encounters the depiction of extra-marital sex — as in *The Guide* — and pre-marital sex — as in *The Painter of Signs* — one knows for certain that through such 'deviations' from the norm Narayan exemplifies the belief that an unsanctified relationship between man and woman would always lead the 'sinners' to frustration. We have Narayan himself viewing the treatment of sex in fiction: "Perhaps I am old fashioned, but I don't think all this coarseness serves any artistic purpose."[5] Narayan would not like to have the privilege as an omnipresent author to be present at the intimate scenes of his characters. He is reported to have said that characters though they are, his men and women must have their own privacy, and he, as an author, is not supposed to take notes sitting by the bedside of his couples.

If one is aware of the implicitly suggested norms and codes and value-judgements in the world of Narayan, then alone can one read logic and reason in the predicament of Raman and Daisy in *The*

Painter of Signs. The sex-obsessed man, flouting the time-honoured sanctity of behaviour, indulging in pre-marital sex, making his pious old aunt quit the household by his sinful conduct, and unceremoniously locking up the family gods in the cupboard to make room for Daisy, would never be given the happiness of marital bliss by the moral novelist. So is the case with Daisy. Daisy is not fond of children and views them as symbols of defeat for her cause. The famous proviso declares that a child has no place in her scheme of life. And to top it all, the concept of 'motherhood' has absolutely no meaning for her. One can't help remembering how Ambika in *The Vendor of Sweets*, pined to have a child and found her status elevated after she had one. Daisy, too, like Raman, was to be deprived of marital happiness for her deviations, and for rebelling agianst cultural norms. The message is clear: the characters conforming to time-honoured norms seem to lead a contented life; and the 'deviants' seem to head towards a frustrating or lonely existence.

Raman's final withdrawal from the mad pursuit of Daisy's love and his acceptance of the ordinary life is also in keeping with the fate of most of Narayan's heroes. Raman may not have experienced the cyclic vision of Srinivas, but he certainly shares with and believes in the latter's philosophy of the "series of births" as he hopes to live with Daisy in their next *Janma*. Raman, in this context seems to voice the very belief of his creator:

> Everything is bound to come out right in the end; if not in this world, at least in other worlds.[6]

Thus, when the novel ends one gets the feeling that Raman remains the same drifter, having grown little as a character. Daisy too, despite her capacity to play Florence Nightingale and Nora rolled into one, remains an artificial character.

In conclusion, it could be pointed out that character delineation in Narayan's novels seems to be influenced subconsciously by Narayan's position as a conformist, and by the typically middle-class milieu he presents as a stage for the drama of the Malgudians. One may not agree with Naipaul's criticism that Narayan's novels are "religious fables", [7] but the view that as a fabulist, Narayan expresses moralistic principles through his characters, sounds reasonable. Although it is extremely difficult to pinpoint the world view of an author, critics of

Narayan seem to agree that what Srinivas in *Mr. Sampath* philosophizes, as he sees the cyclic vision, could be taken as the novelist's own world view. Narayan seems to be prescribing the wisdom of withdrawal and acceptance, "freed from distracting illusions and hysterics".[8] It is here that one may recall Camus' statement that the Incas and the Indians don't rebel for they have their answers in their myths.[9] Thus it may be said that Narayan's firm belief in the pre-ordained scheme of the universe, and his moralistic attitude, have inhibited the growth of his characters. Although as a caricaturist Narayan creates colourful characters, in the final analysis, they remain flat and at times grotesque and, as Graham Greene has said, "rather doubtful".[10]

NOTES

1. Lionel Trilling, 'Emma and the Legend of Jane Austen', in *Beyond Culture: Essays on Literature and Learning* (London: Secker and Warburg, 1966), p.31.

2. R.K. Narayan, *The Painter of Signs* (New York: Viking Penguin, 1976). All subsequent references are to this edition.

3. S. Krishnan, 'A Day with R.K. Narayan', *SPAN* (April 1975), pp. 40–43.

4. Vimala Rao, 'R.K. Narayan's Novelistic Vision — Need for Reappraisal', *The Literary Endeavour* (Jan-June 1982), p.4.

5. S. Krishnan, 'A Day with R.K. Narayan'.

6. R.K. Narayan, 'The World of the Storyteller', *Gods, Demons and Others* (London: Hierfemann, 1965), p.5.

7. V.S. Naipaul, *India: A Wounded Civilization* (London: Andre Deutsch, 1977), p.21.

8. R.K. Narayan, *The Bachelor of Arts* (Mysore: Indian Thought Publications, 1982), p.123.

9. Albert Camus, *The Rebel*, trans. Anthony Bower (Harmondsworth: Penguin, 1986), p.26.

10. Graham Greene, 'Introduction', *The Financial Expert* (Mysore: Indian Thought Publications, 1984), p.viii.

MAKARAND PARANJAPE

Critique of Communism in Raja Rao's *Comrade Kirillov*

It is being increasingly recognized that Raja Rao is the most intellectually demanding of Indian English novelists. His texts have a discursive dimension which makes them essays on some of the major ideological and philosophical systems of our times. This concern with ideas and conceptual systems is typical of Raja Rao's fiction and is noticeable from his earliest works. *Kanthapura* (1938), for instance, is both an exploration and an exposition of Gandhian ideology, worked out through its application to a small, remote South Indian village. *The Serpent and the Rope* (1960) is a compendium of philosophical disquisitions on Vedanta, Bhakti, Hinduism, Christianity, Buddhism, Indian and European history, mysticism, mythology, metaphysics, and so on. In fact, the novel is an exploration of India as an idea in contact with the West; as Rama, the protagonist puts it, "India is not a country like France is, or like England; India is an idea, a metaphysic." [1] *The Cat and Shakespeare* (1965), too, is a Vedantic-Shakespearean parable on the working of self-surrender and grace, or what Govindan Nair calls, "the way of the Cat". Finally, Raja Rao's much awaited, finally released tome, *The Chessmaster and His Moves* (1988), continues and intensifies the debates of *The Serpent and the Rope*. Among other things, it is a dialogue between a Brahmin and a Rabbi, symbolizing the quintessential confrontation between India and the West. In short, Raja Rao is a philosopher-novelist whose works accord a primacy to the evaluation and comprehension of ideas.

It would seem unlikely, then, that a major ideological system such as Communism would escape his interest or scrutiny. Raja Rao's idealist-spiritualist-traditionalist position would naturally be in total antithesis to the materialistic dogmas of Communism. There are, no doubt, stray references to this effect in *The Serpent and the Rope* and in other texts, but it is in *Comrade Kirillov* (1976)[2] that we find a fuller discussion. The text invites added attention especially with the precipitative collapse of Communism in the former USSR and in Eastern Europe. It would be an exaggeration to say that Raja Rao predicted this in *Comrade Kirillov*, but he did portray the defeat of one, largely Stalinist, brand of Indian Communism. The novel satirizes the behaviour of Indian Communists during a specific historical period. Ultimately, Raja Rao's central thesis is that Communism is unsuitable to India because it is incompatible with the essentially spiritual character of the "real" India. Ironically, Raja Rao's views have yet to be proven in India. Communism may have failed in Europe, but is still alive and well in India — of course, in a peculiarly Indian avatar, which has more or less compromised with parliamentary democracy.

Raja Rao's commentary on the mutations of international Communism and on its Indian variations make *Comrade Kirillov* a fascinating text which invites, nay demands, a critical rereading today.

Comrade Kirillov, fourth in order of publication, is the least discussed of Raja Rao's novels. The criticism of the novel has, so far, concentrated on the character of Kirillov, particularly on his "divided consciousness"; on Raja Rao's ironic treatment of it; on the central thematic conflict in the book between Kirillov's faith in Communism and his love for traditional India; on the novel's literary sources and its relation to Dostoevsky's *The Possessed*; and also, to some extent, on the political issues raised in the novel. It is this last area that I would like to explore further here. This paper will consider, first, the importance of politics in the novel; secondly, the political background; and, thirdly, the possible historical sources of Kirillov's character.

It is necessary to recognize that politics is a central rather than peripheral concern in *Comrade Kirillov*. The very first sentence of the novel, "I first met Communism in Kirillov" (p.7), would seem to highlight this, as would a remark made in one of its earliest reviews: "It is difficult to overlook the political overtones especially since the novel is replete with references to the failings in the practice of world communism."³ The novel is, hence, an extended discussion and critique of Communism, especially from an Indian's point of view.

It seems to me that this feature of the novel can be connected with Raja Rao's own involvement in the freedom struggle in India. M.K. Naik in his monograph cryptically refers to this phase in the novelist's career:

> During the "Quit India" movement launched by Mahatma Gandhi in 1942, he (Raja Rao) was associated with the underground activities of the young Socialist leaders.⁴

Because the major events in the novel have to do with this period, it is necessary to understand the situation referred to above in a little more detail. On 9th August, 1942, following the 'Quit India' resolution, Gandhi and the entire leadership of the Congress party which was spearheading the anti-colonial struggle, were arrested and imprisoned. Three months later, on 9th November, six political prisoners, in a daring attempt, escaped from jail. These were the young Socialists, a faction within the Congress, not to be confused with the Communists. It was then that, with the old leaders of the party still in jail, the Socialists first gained recognition as national leaders. Jayaprakash Narayan, Achyut Patwardhan, and Aruna Asaf Ali — the most prominent among them — began to direct the struggle against the British. Evading arrest by going 'underground', they did much to restore the morale of the movement. Presumably, it was with this group that Raja Rao was associated in 1942. Significantly, it was during this period that the Communist Party of India (CPI), as we shall see in detail later, chose to support the British. Raja Rao, being closely involved with these events would have had a firsthand opportunity to examine the functioning of the Indian Communists.

It is therefore clear that an examination of political issues and specific events is crucial to an understanding of the novel and evaluation of the protagonist's character.

*

One of the most important events in Kirillov's life is his paper in support of Britain's war against Germany. This position is quite in opposition to Kirillov's earlier stand on the war, when following the

Hitler-Stalin Pact of 1939, Kirillov had opposed Britain and its "Imperialist war". However, subsequent to Hitler's attack on Russia in 1941, Kirillov, after a period of "seminal psychosis" (p.60), almost akin to the "dark night of the soul" (p.57), undergoes a transformation:

> Somehow this inner conversion appeared almost to have changed his skin — he seemed suddenly to see the skin of Irene on his own wrist and hand, as if by divine compassion. Stalin had made him white — the Indian struggle now entered the international arena, and Marx was justified. (pp.60-61)

Kirillov's thesis, which contains many quotations from Stalin, Lenin, and Marx, is accepted by the party, to his great elation:

> the Party, knowing the scrupulous pertinency of Kirillov's arguments, asked for his final report on the matter. That was one of the greatest days in his life. Messianic emotion surged up his throat, and he went and kissed Irene kindly on her fattening cheeks. (pp.63-64)

This event and Raja Rao's transparently ironic treatment of it, clearly satirizes Kirillov's changing political stance. What is being criticized is Kirillov's and the Communists' expediency and their defence of what is morally and ideologically indefensible. Raja Rao exposes this tendency to rationalize and explain away contradictions as a hallmark of Stalin's anti-democratic regime and, by extension, the craven and imitative self-justifications of the Indian Communists of that time. Significantly, Kirillov's ideological turnabout has been carefully prepared for by his views on two earlier issues: his justification of the Moscow trials in which Stalin liquidated his rivals, and his support of the Hitler-Stalin Pact of 1939.

In the first case, the narrator (R. referred to as "Rama" on p.41 and later revealed to be Raja Rao himself on p.116) goes to Kirillov to get his signature on an appeal on behalf of the the Moscow undertrials:

> Kirillov, I want your signature. It's that a fair trial may be given to the Moscow accused. Here is the manifesto, look. The cause

is good. Your politics is something I do not fully understand. Human suffering, life, birth, death, sickness, marriage, love, God, I understand. I hate violence of all sorts, especially political violence. (p.42)

But Kirillov has no sympathy with such humanitarian views, nor does he have any compunctions regarding violence. Asked how the violence in the USSR and the trials could be justified, he responds with a classic use of the Marxist dialectic:

> If you are weak and on the wrong side — the wrong side for us, as you know, is the weaker side — then you must inevitably go under. (p.44)

Similarly, through Irene's diary, we learn of Kirillov's responses to Stalin's telegram of congratulations to Hitler on Germany's conquest of Poland. Kirillov goes through an elaborate and convoluted process of justification, referring to the *Mantra-Sastra* in the process. The end result is an approval of Stalin's and history's ways:

> Stalin's congratulating Hitler could be reduced by sheer scientific computation to form some seventeen hundred wave-components. Hitler is pleased. Stalin gets his time. That is Marxism. Hitler's message is a psycho-chemical vibration in ether. (p.98)

Both these incidents establish the peculiar morality of Kirillov: it is the morality in which the end justifies the means. Kirillov changes his positions on issues according to party dictates. He justifies himself by believing that his morality is based on irrefutable scientific principles of Marxism: "The only morality is scientific, and this is based on the inexorable laws of cause and effect" (p.37). It is on the basis of this mindset that he makes statements such as the following:

> Man is a biological equation, and Marxism has no traffickings with individuals. All men in Marxism have anonymous names, and death — this last biological act — is an act of sheer surgery against betrayal. (pp.26-27)

Or

> If the biology of selective killing were understood, humanity might yet attain the clear apex of history.... Death, the Moscow deaths, were the antiseptics of history — you kill for the beauty of your eyes. (p.46)

If Kirillov can countenance the Stalinist purges and genocides it is no surprise that he can, with even less soul-searching, support the British during the Quit India movement.

To begin with, Kirillov is completely opposed to the British position in the war. At the height of Hitler's bombing of London, Kirillov is filled with grandiose dreams of the annihilation of the British Empire and of a united and free new world order:

> And once this bloody war was over, the arch of freedom would span the sky from Czechoslovakia to India — why from Greenland to Indonesia. (p.55)

To him, Hitler is an agent of history, God-sent for this purpose:

> Hitler seemed almost an archangel, and his fire had communist ire. Stalin stood mightily behind Hitler — with the backing of the Russian bear the world would be steam-rollered. (p.54)

However, Kirillov's plans are unsettled:

> Kirillov's prognostics this time however, went all wrong... Soviet Russia was attacked by Hitler, and the mechanism of Marxist dialectics changed. (p.57)

The last sentence pithily suggests the aforementioned transformation in Kirillov's position.

Kirillov now finds himself deeply distressed, trying to reconcile his previous anti-imperialist position on the war with this new turn of events:

> Kirillov waited, and waited, with bated breath (his wife surely worried about his health) to know what new turns history

would take. His long intimacy with history had quickly made him into an alien, and he had no illumination — it was the "dark night of the soul." (p.57)

Finally, the directive comes from Stalin himself:

> Stalin had by now given the party directive. We toe the British line. This was a people's war, and India was on the right side — the British side — and he who speaketh against them sells himself to the enemy. (p.59)

To obey Stalin would be to reverse his earlier position. Kirillov reasons with himself thus:

> If Stalin had asked India to side with the British, Stalin had a definite, logical construction on which to base his conclusions. (p. 60)

Then, he experiences his critical illumination:

> he sat himself down, one morning, and wrote a brilliant thesis on the subject. He was inspired like a poet, and his arguments came easily and learnedly. He wrote it all down, handed the document to the right party authority, and looked at his wife for the first time in true sweetness. (p.60)

With this sea change in his position on the war, from virulent opposition to the British to total support, Kirillov suddenly finds himself in favour with the British:

> It was a great, a very great day in the history of India. Comrade Kirillov now became Mr. Padmanabhan Kirillov, his skin shone as on the first day of creation. He could walk up the great steps of any British Secretariat without being looked at askance, and the right passes came in due time. The British Council now turned culture-conscious, invited Kirillov into varied assemblies, and before his receptive audiences Kirillov developed astonishing labour theories on the people's war. The Indian Communist Weekly changed its name from *National Front* to *People's War*, and versatile writers exposed the great popular enthusiasm

wrought by Soviet Policy in the working classes of Bombay and Calcutta. (p.61)

These events, namely, Kirillov's opposition to the war, his subsequent support of it, and finally, his finding favour with the British, reflect very closely the politics of the Communist Party of India during the same period. In fact, the parallels are so close as to suggest that Raja Rao was using Kirillov's story as an allegorical critique of Communism in general and the conduct of the CPI in particular.

The facts of the case are so well known that I shall only provide a brief summary from R.C. Majumdar's *History of the Freedom Movement in India*:

> The Communists, all over the world, outside Russia, were puzzled by the Stalin-Hitler Pact in August 1939. But they had to obey instructions from Moscow. So Hitler ceased to be a Fascist menace, and became a friend of peace, while England and France were the imperialist war-mongers.
>
> But as soon as Germany invaded Russia on 22 June, 1941 all these were changed as if by the wand of a magician. The authorities of International communism demanded that the CPI must support the British war efforts as they contributed to the defence of the Soviet Union, the Fatherland of Communism... The Imperial War became overnight a People's War by the magic wand of Communism.
>
> The official attitude towards the CPI also underwent a complete change. The Communist leaders were set free, and on 24 July, 1942, the ban against the Communist Party was lifted. Henceforth the CPI functioned as a legal party and enjoyed the favours of the Government of India. Persons kept in detention on account of Communist activities were used by the Government as a counterpoise to the Congress. The spectacle was thus witnessed in India — the leftist Communist Party being antinational and pro-imperial, and eating up the very words by which they had so long incited the people against the imperial and war-monger British.[5]

These events, if not the above interpretation of them, are corroborated by the standard works on the subject.

The direction of Raja Rao's satire is seen in how closely Kirillov's unbounded devotion to the USSR resembles actual documents of the CPI.

> Soviet defeats were turned into Marxist mannerisms of inevitable success — the working classes must and would inevitably win — and the battle for India was fought within the walls of Stalingrad. One day when the Indian bourgeoise would be liquidated, Stalingrad would shape a statue for great Stalin, Leader and Father of the Soviet Land. (pp.61-62)

Compare the above passage from the novel with the following excerpt from the CPI's Party Letter of 13 December 1941:

> the attitute of the Communist Parties to war is always determined not by any national or local considerations but by the single consideration: international unity and action of the world proletariat to strike at world imperialism, to defend the Socialist Fatherland.[6]

The language of Kirillov's internal monologue, thus, echoes the Party Letter; Raja Rao shows how propaganda beclouds an individual's judgement. The contradictions in Kirillov's character are deftly exposed.

It is not surprising, therefore, to find Kirillov sticking to the Russian line even when events in India do not go as forecast. Gandhi's Quit India movement evoked an enthusiastic response in India, while those who continued to support the British lost ground. Yet Kirillov's faith in his Soviet mentors remains undiminished:

> Whatever the peculiarity of the Indian situation, Russia was wedged to her promise — this shall be a people's war and the Allies must be sustained. Stalin had studied the problem, his decision had been made. One need not worry him again — he was busy with other matters. The party line was now given: and it was not to be changed for the moment. Kirillov found Stalin uncomfortable — but as a Marxist leader, Stalin had, of course, the right perspective. (p.64)

The quotation, through its ironic tone, clearly underscores Kirillov's blind faith in Stalin.

By this comparison between the actual political events of the period and Kirillov's attitudes to them, it is clear that the latter reflect the positions and policies of the CPI. The most notable of these parallels are :

a. The attitude to the Moscow trials.
b. The position on the Hitler-Stalin Pact of 1939.
c. The opposition to Britain's imperialist war.
d. Support of Britain's "People's war".
e. The political advantages of the shift in position
f. The reasons for an unswerving loyalty to the Soviet line.

Thus, *Comrade Kirillov*, in addition to being an ironic portrait of a conflict-ridden Indian expatriate intellectual, also offers a critique of the political fluctuations and manoeuvres of the CPI during the 1930s and 1940s. Raja Rao is indirectly exposing what he sees as the inconsistencies, contradictions, and self-deceptions of Communism as it is actually practised by its adherents, particularly of the pre-Independence Indian variety. The novel, therefore, has historical and ideological ramifications beyond what may commonly be perceived.

Besides being a commentary and an allegorical portrayal of actual events in India, the novel is significant as a criticism of Stalinism in particular and the hegemony of master discourses in general. Although Raja Rao's critique is grounded in what is clearly a nationalist-spiritual-liberal-humanitarian tradition, he is quick to identify the lapses, excesses, errors, and contradictions within Communism. For him, Communism is wrong not so much because it is materialist-historicist, but because of its distortions of rationality. It represents human engineering gone awry. That he could articulate his opposition so clearly in an era in which the eventual collapse of Communism was not even a remote possibility is remarkable.

Raja Rao's, and by implication, history's, verdict on Kirillov and what he stands for is curt and brief, quite in contrast to the indulgent tone in which the latter is ordinarily treated:

> Comrade Kirillov played an anonymous role in international history. 1942 came and with it the great Indian revolution. Churchill was shaken, and though Britain prolonged her commitments for another four years, India was lost to them in

1942. The Communist Party backed Britain, and lost their 1917. Mahatma Gandhi won. He would always win, for he knew India. (p.69)

Symbolically, Kirillov never returns to India; instead he is last heard of in Peking (p.121).

*

Finally, I would like to address the question of the sources of the character of Kirillov. Naik has already examined the relation of the book to its chief literary source, Dostoevsky's *The Possessed* in which the original Kirillov may be found. In this connection, it only needs to be pointed out that Raja Rao would sometimes seem to confuse Kirillov with Shatov, another character in *The Possessed*. For instance, in Raja Rao's novel, Kirillov is spoken of as rushing to the midwife, delirious with joy, when he finds out that his wife Marie is pregnant with another man's child (p.49). In the original of Dostoevsky, it is Shatov, not Kirillov, whose wife Marie is pregnant with another man's child. Similar references elsewhere in the novel have been corrected by an insertion of the phrase "like Shatov" (pp.25,90), thereby making Raja Rao's Kirillov an amalgam of both Kirillov and Shatov of Dostoevksy.

Besides this literary source, Kirillov, as pointed out by others (see Dey[7] and Srivastava[8] for example), closely resembles Rama, the protagonist of *The Serpent and the Rope* in several ways including the Brahminical background, the philosophic disposition, foreign wife, expatriate status, preoccupations with India, interest in the Albegensian heresy, chanting of Sankara, and so on. Moving from fictive to factual sources, Narasingh Srivastava is of the opinion that Kirillov closely resembles Raja Rao himself. Actually, it would be more accurate to say that Ramaswamy, Kirillov, and R., the narrator of *Comrade Kirillov*, are all versions of a prototype loosely derived from Raja Rao's own experience.

Other historical sources have been suggested by V.V. Badve[9] in a review-article on the book: "So we have in Kirillov J. Krishnamurti, Krishna Menon (and perhaps M.N. Roy) all rolled into one." The first option is unlikely because Krishnamurti, clearly, is mentioned as a separate character in the novel (pp.9-14) and Kirillov is supposed to have been his disciple. Besides, there are no major resemblances between the two.

The second option has been discussed by Naik:

> Raja Rao's Kirillov appears, at least in some significant respects to be modelled upon the noted Indian statesman V.K. Krishna Menon, who like Kirillov, was a brilliant, versatile and voluble South Indian expatriate. He too, like Raja Rao's hero, came early under the spell of Mrs. Annie Besant, and was sent abroad for education as a young man, having been earmarked for becoming a pillar of the Theosophist movement in India. Menon, however, became similarly associated with the British Labour Party. Unlike Kirillov however, he never married and never became a Communist...[10]

The crucial difference pointed out by Naik himself, that Menon never became a Communist, makes this an unlikely resemblance. After all, almost the entirety of Kirillov's character derives, as the title suggests, from his being a Communist.

The third possibility, that of M.N. Roy as a source, needs to be examined more seriously. Curiously enough, there are several parallels; first, Roy, whose original name was Narendranath Bhattacharya, like Kirillov, came from a Brahmin family. Secondly, like Kirillov's earlier devotion to Theosophy, Roy was an ardent nationalist, deeply influenced by the religious ideas of leaders like Swami Vivekananda. Thirdly, like Kirillov, he changed his name to Manabendra Nath Roy. Fourthly, he too 'converted' to Communism like Kirillov. Fifthly, he married a European. Sixthly, he too wrote a paper, which was widely acclaimed, for the Second Congress of the Communist International in 1920. Seventhly, he supported the British during the war. Finally, he too had an ambivalent attitude to Gandhi and other Congress leaders, and he too, like Kirillov, went to China for some time.

Though these similarities exist, the differences, too, abound. The chief of these is that M.N. Roy was an intellectual heavyweight, taken seriously both in India and abroad, not an object of amusement like Kirillov. Also, he was actively involved in Indian politics, unlike Kirillov who remains an expatriate. Finally, Roy moved away from Communism when he found that it had betrayed its ideals. He proposed a new philosophy called Radical Humanism instead. Kirillov, of course, is more of a follower than a leader and never moves away from Communism.

There is one more possible source for Kirillov which needs to be examined. Kirillov bears a close resemblance to Virendranath Chattopadhyaya (1880-1942), one of Sarojini Naidu's younger brothers. He was a revolutionary whose portrait can be found in Martyrs' Hall, Calcutta. He was an exile who worked against imperialism all his life. Like Kirillov, he was from a Brahmin family. His major work was his thesis on India and world imperialism, co-authored with G.A. Luganin and P. Khankhoje, presented at the Third Congress of the Communist International. The thesis was sent to Lenin and he even responded to it in a letter dated July 8, 1921. There are other references to Chattopadhyaya in the *Collected Works of Lenin*. Chattopadhyaya was not married, but had a long-term relationship with the Communist leader, Agnes Sedly. His later years were lonely and poverty-stricken.

Overall, it would seem that Kirillov is based not on any single individual, but is an amalgam of various people, real and fictional. I have, however, tried to show that there is a historical type on which Kirillov has been based — the Indian Communist of Brahmin ancestry, married to a European, and in exile from India.

*

After trying to trace the historical and political background of the novel, the question of who Kirillov is and what he represents needs to be addressed. As I have shown, on one level, Kirillov is an expatriate Indian intellectual and an Indian Communist in exile. But he is also an idea and a symbol. He is the vehicle of the author's discussion and criticism of Communism in idea and practice, somewhat similar to Dostoevsky's symbolic use of characters in *The Possessed* to explore the psychological and political bases of the revolutionary movements of the later part of 19th century Russia. That Raja Rao employs Kirillov not only as an individual character, but also as a political and psychological type is, no doubt, amply clear from the entire thrust of the book. But there are, in addition, some direct statements in the text which support such a claim: "There are a million Kirillovs — Indian, Chinese, Albanian, Egyptian, North-Siberian, Guadeloupian, Greenlandian, Swedish, Norwegian, Polish, Portuguese" (p.49). Kirillov represents, then, not only the practice of Indian Communism of a certain period in particular, but many facets of international Communism in general. He is Raja Rao's vehicle for a critique against the entire ideological apparatus of Stalinism.

In the Indian context, Kirillov is the antithesis of the thesis that is, by implication, Mahatma Gandhi. The latter, for Raja Rao, is the "true" Indian and the modern representative of traditional India. In this dialectical struggle, there is no Hegelian synthesis at the end; rather, the result is the triumph of the Gandhian-Brahminical thesis. For, as the author says, "Mahatma Gandhi had won. He would always win, for he knew India" (p.69).

The defeat of what Kirillov stands for is reinforced in the concluding section of the book when the narrator initiates Kirillov's son into the mysteries of India: "A few days later Kamal and I left on a pilgrimage to the South. I wanted to show Kamal my India" (p.122). If Kirillov is the symbol of an Indian Communism that is alienated from the "true" spirit of India, the reclamation of his symbolic offspring by India at the end once again underscores the ultimate inefficacy and reabsorption of such a Communism. The novel ends with Kamal's reintegration into the orthodox and traditional India of the author:

> When evening came again, and the wind had totally fallen, I dressed Kamal in sacred silk, gave him his silver waist-band, and sandal on his face, showed him to Mother Kanyakumari. Between the lamps and the bright Goddess, we heard the leaping adoration of the ninth moon ocean.

Raja Rao's portrayal of Communism through the vacillating and divided character of Kirillov may, perhaps, be an unfair or exaggerated representation. Yet it is based on sufficient historical evidence to be taken seriously. The only way to refute it would be to question his basic premise about the 'true' nature of the Indian mind and culture. If, indeed, India is a country whose unique and special orientation is spiritual, then the fate to which he consigns Communism is unavoidable. However, it is possible to argue that India is not a culture and civilization which is primarily spiritual, but rather a plural space open to various contesting world views and ideologies. No matter how much the spiritual might be construed to be the dominant strand of this culture — for such has been the view of not just Western orientalists, but of a long line of significant Indian thinkers from Rammohan Roy to Vinoba Bhave — it cannot and must not pretend to be the sole or primary one.

Hence, there is ample room for conflicting philosophies and ideologies, whether materialist or spiritualist, in India. If so, then India can provide a hospitable climate for the flourishing of a multiplicity of viewpoints, one of which has certainly been Communism. In fact, in spite of its collapse in Europe, an entire spectrum of Left ideologies flourishes in India. The CPM, one such Communist Party in India, has even been ruling Bengal for many years, having won its position not through the bullet but through the ballot.

NOTES

1. Raja Rao, *The Serpent and the Rope* (London: John Murray, 1960), p.376.

2. Raja Rao, *Comrade Kirillov* (New Delhi: Orient Paperbacks, 1976). All subsequent references are to this edition.

3. P.K. Rajan, 'Introducing *Comrade Kirillov*', in *Littcritt*, 3.1 (June 1977), pp. 51-54.

4. M.K. Naik, *Raja Rao* (New York: Twayne, 1976. Revised rpt. Bombay: Blackie and Son, 1982), p.20.

5. R.C. Majumdar, *History of the Freedom Movement in India*, Vol.III (Calcutta: Firma KLM, 1977), p.569.

6. Quoted in Arun Shourie, 'The Great Betrayal', *The Illustrated Weekly of India* (April 1-7, 1984), pp.6-13.

7. Esha Dey, 'Raja Rao's India: The Axis of *Comrade Kirillov*, an Anti-Novel', in *Commonwealth Quarterly*, 5.20(1980-81), pp. 24-43.

8. Narasingh Srivastava, 'Raja Rao's *Comrade Kirillov*: The dilemma of a divided consciousness', in *Journal of Commonwealth Literature*, 16.1, pp. 8-15.

9. V.V. Badve, 'Raja Rao's *Comrade Kirillov*', in *New Quest*, Vol.14 (March-April 1979), pp. 121-128.

10. M.K. Naik, 'Raja Rao's *Comrade Kirillov*', in *The Indian Journal of English Studies*, Vol.XXI (1981-82), pp. 107-116.

SHIRISH V CHINDHADE

The triumph of timeless India: Rama Mehta's *Inside the Haveli*

Like any successful work of art, Rama Mehta's novel *Inside the Haveli*[1] has many layers of themes, each of which can be amplified into an independent study. For instance, it is usually read as a poignant sociological study of the gradually changing status of the New Woman in India, an account of her educational development and consequent economic independence. It can also be taken as an absorbing example of 'feminist' writing where a young girl is the protagonist — something that is still somewhat infrequent in the Indian novel in English. One more peculiarity about the story is that the entire cast of female characters conspicuously outnumbers the male ones. Still another point of view is that it is a convincing *Bildungsroman* with the protagonist having to conduct a number of experiments in living in a world that is not readily conducive to such a spirit of experimentation and exploration. The book also has a great beauty of design which evolves chiefly through parallels, contrasts, metaphors and symbols.

The novel is all these things and more because, except for the theme of *Bildungsroman*, the above descriptions seem to focus chiefly on the physical and perhaps the intellectual dimensions of the feminine world. This seems inadequate and superficial. Therefore, this paper attempts to see whether the work also focuses on another important dimension of a woman's personality, namely woman as a 'normal' human being with spiritual depth, a moral vision, a potential that helps her to transcend worldly and intellectual experiences, eventually enabling her to emerge as the true image of eternal India.

Novelists, both male and female, have tried to present images of woman varying from Durga to *devdasi*, one a sentimental idealization, the other a popular cabaret dancer. It is possible to see a rather different, new and justly sublime, image of woman in the work under discussion, which ostensibly presents a sociologist's realistic account of a large section of Indian society. The region selected for this study is Rajasthan with the well-delineated, specific locale of the city of Udaipur and its traditional *havelis* in which the position of women seems to be relegated to a secondary citizenship; a world in which the birth of a female child is announced apologetically and accepted reluctantly.

This reality is represented through the experiences of the various female characters in the story, with Gita as the chief instrument of consciousness. For instance, when a child is born to Lakshmi, a maid-servant in the *haveli*, her husband, Gangaram, guesses correctly that it must be a girl. Had it been a boy, Sanju, the midwife, would have come out in the rain and thunder, shouting "It's a boy, it's a boy. Give me money" (p.5). Gita, the new daughter-in-law in the *haveli*, Jiwan Nivas, is also in a state of accouchement and the servants keep guessing at the sex of the child. Gangaram remarks, "Of course, she will get a boy. The rich always get what they want" (p.5). Gita, who is brought up and educated in the free and uninhibited world of Bombay, is constrained to unlearn many things in order to confront the altogether different world of Udaipur. We are told that she is spontaneous, lively and has "not been taught to stint in giving affection," nor to keep her feelings concealed. In fact, her parents had encouraged her to speak her mind, and there is a childlike enthusiasm in everything she does and says. But once in the *haveli*, her mother-in-law keeps reminding her of "the importance of reticence" (p.28). Her education begins anew and one of the first lessons she has to learn with much pain and effort, is that to be a woman means to be in bondage of one kind or the other.

Situations and events keep contributing new lessons to her knowledge of life. For instance, when Lakshmi grumbles about being forced into marriage, Pari the chief maid comforts and consoles her thus:

> Look at me; though I have been a widow almost all my life, I am still not free from my in-laws... I never have a penny left

after the demands of my in-laws. And what do I get from them? Nothing. Not even a blouse. But I don't complain. We all have to accept fate. There is no escape from that. (p.9)

These are almost prophetic words for Gita, for she too has to accept her fate by staying in the *haveli*. Another senior maid, Dhapu, also remonstrates with Lakshmi: "Look at you with your head uncovered. Were it any other man, he would beat you... which man can put up with a wife who does not make him comfortable?" (p.10). Thus what is expected of a woman is an unquestioning, meek acceptance of a constricting tradition that stretches as far back as the time of the ancient sage Manu, the giver of law, who declares in the *Manusmriti*:

> *Pita rakshati kaumarye*
> *Bharta rakshati yauwane*
> *Sthavire putrah rakshanti*
> *Na stri swatantrymarhti*

(The father protects a woman in her childhood, the husband in her youth and the sons in her old age. Hence, a woman is unworthy of freedom.)

The words of the two maids are both an exhortation and a warning to Gita of the ways that every (Indian) woman is expected to reconcile herself to. This is, however, only the epistemological shell of the story, rather hard to crack, but the kernel inside seems perhaps worth the trouble. Now the Indian female ideal is the cow, proverbially praised for her divinity and docility. Dhapu wants Lakshmi to follow this ideal and thereby immerse her total identity in the drift of the humdrum life of the *haveli*. Both Gita and Lakshmi (her second self), face essentially the same problem: "How would such a girl learn to live in the constricted atmosphere of a world of women, to give her elders the traditional deference?" (p.13). Lakshmi vehemently and rashly refuses to be the proverbial cow and submit to coercive customs. She is too proud and restive to suffer the slightest injustice and repression, the 'slings and arrows of outrageous fortune'. Gita, on the other hand, also wants to revolt and retaliate but her formal education, her upbringing, her urbanity, and her initial embarrassment caused by the new atmosphere, have practically removed the sting and instilled a subdued tolerance. In effect, Lakshmi translates her verbal protest into a desperate action and finally suffers ignominy, whereas Gita continues to be 'willing to wound and yet afraid to strike' but finally attains dignity, equanimity and liberation by not striking.

The epistemological shell can be split further: Can Gita adjust to a constricting situation and atmosphere? How? How would an educated girl like her be approved of by Ajay's family? How is it possible for Gita to win her freedom in a place where freedom seems to mean confinement? Is freedom at all possible in a tradition where to be a woman means to be a prisoner and a mere chattel? Gita's growth and metamorphosis from a restlesss, spontaneous, irascible young girl into a mature, happy, composed woman lies in the solutions to the problems just mentioned above. Such solutions are not easy to come by. They come after severe trials and tribulations, restrictions, continence, humiliations, constricting manners, mores and taboos. Traditionally, this is *Sadhana*. Even the slightest departure from the norm, any immature waywardness, any desperate and defiant deed is sure to land one in interminable trouble, as is demonstrated in the case of Lakshmi. Her life in the *haveli* was ridden with restrictions and inhibitions but it was also securely rooted. Her woes begin from the day she gives up the *haveli* in defiance and desperation. She becomes derelict and deprived, merely drifting from one master to another, now a *panwala*, then a tailor. It is reported that she is "not leading an honourable life " (p. 69). The world thinks that "she is a widow who has no one in the world... she is a little out of her mind" (p.145). In all certainty, she would have become Pari (i.e., the chief maid) in due course after her "penance". However, Lakshmi loses through desperation and defiance what Pari has won through patience and deference.

This is significant in the epistemological context. Lakshmi's suffering emphatically underlines the necessity of a fine coordination between thought and action, which is possible through formal education. It is this education that differentiates Gita from Lakshmi. The *haveli*, which is the seat of the well-entrenched traditional culture, asserts that "even an educated girl can be moulded" (p.26), perhaps because there is a presupposition that good education is expected to instil adaptability, a sense of accommodation, the capacity to integrate and assimilate old and new ideas and habits. That is why everyone in the *haveli*, from Dhapu, Lakshmi and Pari to the mother-in-law, contributes significantly to Gita's moulding and growth; Lakshmi cannot be subjected to such a shaping because of her inherent faults and the absence of the deterrent and corrective force of education. In her case, the shaping spirit is embodied in her husband who, being rather wishy-washy and self-immersed, is incapable of exerting a lasting moderating influence on her. Gita's shaping spirits are her mother and father-in-law, and her husband. The mother-in-law may look mild, frail and bird-like, but she holds herself erect. She walks with "indescribable self-confidence and exudes strength and dignity as if she were naturally born to command" (p.26). She obviously personifies the traditional culture and prestige of the *haveli* which Gita must necessarily inherit in due course, but not without undergoing a great deal of suffering. The results are startling. The immature, restless, romantic, irascible girl is ultimately competent and ready to take command of the *haveli* while the recalcitrant, licentious Lakshmi comes to grief and is reduced to becoming an opprobrious nonentity.

Thus another truth that dawns on Gita is that defiance is injurious and deference is rewarding. Lakshmi is disinherited from a rich, high tradition through defiance but Gita becomes one with it and attains status and peace through deference. She is told at an earlier stage, "In order to become one with the family, one must first listen to one's elders" (p.96). Listening to one's elders traditionally means observing one's dharma. Lakshmi fails to observe it because of her defiance and wrath that breed rashness and catastrophe. The observance of one's dharma is essential because dharma teaches right action which, in turn, assures liberation (moksha) from suffering and sorrow.[2] Lakshmi must suffer, be unhappy and be condemned ultimately like the Kauravas who failed to observe their dharma. On the other hand, Gita learns to observe it through *sadhana* and is regenerated, awakened into a new life redolent with a sweet sense of fulfilment, dignity and freedom. The *Bhagavadgita* underlines this in the following line: *Swe swe karmanyabhirata, sansiddhir labhate narah* (one engrossed in his dharma attains beatitude). Through her experiences and experiments a subtle sense of "belonging" evolves in Gita which is symbolically intensified in her mini-school in the *haveli*. It may be considered as a metaphor of her epistemological leap forward that, like herself, she must educate the others too. Besides filling her vacant days with a meaningful, creative occupation, the school also fosters a sense of understanding and forgiveness in her and she suddenly begins to love the large, empty rooms of the *haveli*. They no longer look unfriendly and haunted. "As the children and woman learned to read and write, Gita got a deeper understanding of poverty" (p.130). Like everyone else, the children too are changing. They sweep clean the cobwebs in the *haveli* — obviously a significant suggestive gesture.

The decisive moment of epiphany dawns in Gita's life when the senior master of the haveli dies and the "keys" are handed over to her.

> Her heart filled with pride and admiration for the man who was the father of her husband. All of a sudden, she realised what real greatness meant. He was like a towering tree under which the family sheltered. It was from him that everyone got their nourishment. (p.207)

This detail is rich in suggestion as it marks the completion of Gita's education after having assimilated in herself the ancient triple doctrine of *da* (give), *damyata* (restrain), *dayadhwam* (have mercy).

It is at this stage that the grand paradox central to the *Vedas* and the *Bhagavadgita* emerges: There is loss in possession and gain in renunciation. In trying to possess her worldly freedom, Gita initially loses her equanimity; it is only when she renounces pride and private desires that she becomes aware of her inordinate gain. If one abides by form, norm and etiquette, one can attain the greatest freedom. In other words, self-restraint becomes the best form of freedom while orgiastic liberty is the worst type of incarceration. This is dramatized through the role reversals of Gita and Lakshmi. Lakshmi who is initially an insider eventually becomes *persona non grata* in the *haveli* but with Gita the reverse happens. Gita feels happy and emancipated through abnegation, service and self-knowledge. To borrow a phrase from T.S. Eliot, she works out her "salvation with diligence".[3] Like Hans Andersen's ugly duckling, she understands the blissful truth about herself: that she is not a mere "chattel" (p.15), but the veritable chief — the *grihini* — of Jeevan Niwas; and the *grihini* it is who makes the home. How can the *haveli* be a prison for one who has realized that it is really a hermitage, an Abode of Life (Jeevan

Niwas)? How can Gita be unhappy when she has realized the truth that true fulfilment lies in living for others, in doing one's duty to others? She is like the senior master of Jeevan Niwas who, like a huge banyan tree, sacrificed his life so that the *haveli* may get nourishment.

The writer has used suitable 'architecture' to get across this pithy message. The book opens with rains, thunder and midnight darkness, appropriately foreshadowing Gita's ignorant struggle; it ends with the rising sun symbolic of life and Gita's enlightenment, reminding us of the ancient prayer: *tamaso ma jyotirgamaya*. The key concept here seems to be that of renunciation. The following two quotations help to summarize the argument. Meenakshi Mukherjee mentions one quotation from the *Bhagavadgita* given on the last page of B. Rajan's novel, *The Dark Dancer*.

> He who seeks freedom,
> Thrusts fear aside,
> Thrusts aside anger,
> and puts off desire;
>   Truly that man
> is made free forever.

She argues that

> Renunciation has always been an Indian ideal of life, be it renunciation of worldly goods and possessions, or the renunciation of selfish motives, passion and emotional bondage. Like all ideals it is a distinctly difficult condition, attainable only by a few. In real life one hardly ever sees an ideal realised. But in literature it is not impossible to create a credible individual by the complete realisation of all the fragmentary attributes one sees in different human beings. Such a character will adhere to the ideals of non-attachment, conquest of senses, and selfless love towards all humanity.[4]

In a different context S.K. De has examined the reasons behind this urge to create such characters:

> The external world had never possessed any inherent interest to the naturally stoical and idealistic Hindu. A majestic common

sense, and rich feeling for the concrete facts and forces of human nature and human life, a sense of enjoyment of good things of earth, a passion of energy and action are traits which foster material civilization but which are antagonistic to Hindu ideas of placid contentment, to the insensibility, amazement and ecstasy of religious devotion, to the wishfulness and pathos of spiritual desires.[5]

These seem to be apt answers to critics and objectors of every sort.

NOTES

1. Rama Mehta, *Inside the Haveli* (Delhi: Arnold-Heinemann, 1977). All subsequent references are to this edition.

2. The *Mahabharata* stresses the observance of Dharma as follows:
   Dharmadarthshcha Kamashcha
   Sa dharma kim na sevyate?
   (Since all achivements, fulfilments — and the consequent *moksha* — are guaranteed in the observance of Dharma, why, then, not abide by it?)

3. T.S. Eliot, 'The Cocktail Party', *The Complete Poems and Plays of T.S. Eliot* (London: Faber and Faber, 1969), p.411.

4. Meenakshi Mukherjee, *The Twice-Born Fiction* (Delhi: Arnold-Heinemann, 1971), pp.99-100.

5. S.K. De, *History of Bengali Literature – The Nineteenth Century 1800-1925* as quoted by Dorothy M. Spencer in 'Indian Society, Culture and Fiction', in *Indian Fiction in English* (Philadelphia: University of Pennsylvania Press, 1960), pp. 9-10.

VASANT A SHAHANE

Fictional montage in Anita Desai's *Fire on the Mountain*

Anita Desai's art of fiction may be compared, in my view, with the artist's endeavour to create a sophisticated montage in an aesthetic form. Montage may be defined as the art or the process of making a composite picture by bringing together into a single composition, or art-form, different pictures and arranging them in an aesthetic sequence so that they form a blended whole with a distinct identity of its own. This generalized definition of a montage admirably fits in with, and governs the pattern of, Anita Desai's fiction — the process of its creativity, its development and its aesthetic projection. It is also a kind of fictional mosaic unfolding the process of drawing pictures and fitting them into a total design. While the concept of the mosaic, emanating from the Muses, is primarily artistic and pictorial, the idea of the montage is aesthetic as well as dramatic, projecting, among other things, the dramatic and spiritual crisis of the soul.

Anita Desai's fifth novel, *Fire on the Mountain*[1] pervasively demonstrates the novelist's basic technique of fiction as montage. It is indeed a subtle 'technique', as a process of discovery, a mode of projecting a vision. In fact, it is a craft which cannot be dissociated from the constituents of the art of fiction, such as the rhythm, the prophecy, the portrayal of individual and social reality, and the visionary quality of the imagination.

Fire on the Mountain is a distinctive novel primarily because it is a mosaic of many patterns, a texture of many images drawn from botanical and zoological sources. In no other novel of Desai's has this mosaic of the human and the natural, the past and the present, the individual and the social, the inner and the outer, the movable and the immovable, the transient and the eternal been portrayed with such great power and poignancy almost bordering on a tragic sense of life. Thus, technique becomes discovery through contrasted conditions of human consciousness pitted against an apathetic social reality, and the unfolding of barriers in man's quest for the realization of ideal harmony.

The mosaic slowly becomes a montage as it unfolds the spiritual drama of Nanda Kaul's inner being, her soul, her striving for isolation, loneliness and withdrawal. The mosaic-like montage is often achieved through the unfolding of opposites, revealed in the coexistence of opposed valuations of life, such as, for example, the modes of involvement and detachment, movement and stillness, privacy and familial togetherness, fulfilling one's self and adhering to society's moral code of duty. These contrasts are woven into the fabric of the novel through an imagistic pattern which finally attains a symbolic accentuation. The narrative content in *Fire on the Mountain* is lowkey, and is encased in its dominant form, the delicate texture of the montage.

Fire on the Mountain is divided into three parts: 'Nanda Kaul at Carignano'; 'Baka comes to Carignano'; 'Ila Das leaves Carignano'. While these three parts are named after the three main characters in the fictional narrative, Nanda Kaul's house on the ridge in Kasauli plays almost an equal part in the lives of all three of them and the extension of their consciousness. The house, Carignano, has a history of its own and its starkness, barrenness, and its apricot trees are all part of Nanda Kaul's expanding or contracting consciousness. The house in the hill-station at Kasauli was built by a Colonel Macdougall in 1843 for his wife, Alice, and their seven sick children. The account of their life, death, and the burial of their seven children, and of their cemetery was written by the Colonel himself. It is filled with pathos and pain. It ends with a description of the house itself. The Macdougalls, too, were later consigned to the earth and their house stood empty for quite some time. A terrific thunderstorm had blown off its green roof consisting of corrugated iron sheets, which fell in the valley below killing a coolie on the spot. Later, the house passed on to other occupants, the pastor of the church, Miss Appleby and a host of other 'maiden ladies' until it came to be owned by Nanda Kaul in 1947.

Carignano embodies the spirit of the place, which is absorbed by its occupants, including Nanda Kaul, whose expanding horizons of consciousness seem to share the linkage of the house with the process of ageing, barrenness, loneliness, decay and death. The very first sentence of the first chapter introduces Nanda Kaul to the reader:

> Nanda Kaul paused under the pine trees to take in their scented sibilance and listen to the cicadas fiddling invisibly under the mesh of pine needles when she saw the postman slowly winding his way along the Upper Mall. She had not gone out to watch for him, did not want him to stop at Carignano, had no wish for letters.(p.3)

Nanda Kaul's close link with Nature, the pine trees and the cicadas, her intense disinclination to receive any letters, and her irritation at the very sight of the postman unfold her principal attributes in relation to the natural and the human world.

> Everything she wanted was here, at Carignano, in Kasauli. Here on the ridge of the mountain, in this quiet house. It was the place, and the time of life, that she had wanted and prepared for all her life — as she realised on her first day at Carignano, with a great, cool flowering of relief and at last she had it. She wanted no one and nothing else. Whatever else came, or happened here would be unwelcome intrusion and distraction. (p.3)

Nanda Kaul had reached such a stage in her life — old age, infirmity, resignation, loneliness, withdrawal, non-involvement — that she felt much closer to the trees than to any human being.

> She was grey, tall and thin and her silk sari made a sweeping, shivering sound and she fancied she could merge with the pine trees and be mistaken for one. To be a tree, no more and no less, was all she was prepared to undertake. (p.4)

The postman climbed the hill, delivered a letter to Nanda Kaul, which intruded in her private, lonely world. It was from Nanda's daughter, Asha. Asha had written about Tara, who was married to a diplomat, Rakesh, who had been ill-treating her. It was a painful domestic quarrel. However, Rakesh had got a new posting in Geneva and Asha desired that Tara should go with him "to give him another chance" (p.14). However, the main problem in this arrangement was Raka, Tara's daughter, who had just recovered from typhoid, and was very much in need of the fresh air of the hills to recuperate.

The letter seemed to Nanda Kaul a significant reminder of duty to the family and the need to accommodate Raka at Carignano. However, it was also a signal of intrusion into the privacies of Nanda's lonely world. Her world of detachment was up against the demanding tide of involvement; her solitary existence was now faced with the possible invasion of her privacy by a child signifying family duty and the need to take care of close relations.

Nanda Kaul tried to recollect the figure of Raka and her environment and also the moments of tender care bestowed on children, and a host of associated memories flashed before her mind's eye. She remembered the days when she had tended her own children and grandchildren — Asha, Tara, Vina — and their offspring too. The prospect of Raka's arrival at Carignano filled Nanda Kaul with a little apprehension, and irritation. "How could she sleep with someone else in the house?" (p.35). She began to visualize her duties to Raka and her well-being and how she would have to urge her to eat eggs and spinach, to caution her against scorpions, and also to entertain her by telling her stories, nursery rhymes, etc.

Part II of *Fire on the Mountain* narrates the story of Raka's arrival and Nanda Kaul's reaction to her great-granddaughter's postures and activities. Nanda Kaul stood near the apricot trees to welcome Raka, and the pine trees "stood bending and twisting extravagantly in the wind as though miming welcome in a modern satiric ballet". Nanda Kaul was taken aback by Raka's sense of independence, her instinct to be herself, and her tendency towards being solitary, her desire to be stubbornly 'alone'.

> But it gave her an increased sense of Raka's dependence on her, Nanda Kaul. She was not sure if it was poignant, ironical or merely irritating that Raka herself remained totally unaware of her dependence, was indeed as independent and solitary as ever. Watching her wandering amongst the rocks and agaves of the ravine, tossing a horse chestnut rhythmically from hand to

hand, Nanda Kaul wondered if she at all realised how solitary she was. She certainly never asked nor bothered to see if there were a letter for her, or news. Solitude never disturbed her. She was the only child Nanda Kaul had ever known who preferred to stand apart and go off and disappear to being loved, cared for and made the centre of attention. The children, Nanda Kaul had known had wanted only to be such centres: Raka alone did not. (pp 79-80)

This extraordinary attribute of Raka makes her appear almost a kindred spirit to Nanda Kaul. Raka fitted into the atmosphere of Carignano as an 'uninvited mouse' or a 'cricket'. Raka's affinity with the spirit of the place makes Nanda Kaul think:

Would she own it herself one day, Carignano? Nanda Kaul wondered, lashing her fingers together over her chest. Ought she to leave it to Raka? Certainly it belonged to no one else, had no meaning for anyone else. Raka alone understood Carignano, knew what Carignano stood for — she alone valued that, Nanda Kaul knew. (p.80)

Chapter fifteen relates the story of the visit to Tibet by Nanda Kaul's father — the entire event recollected while she and Raka are having tea. Nanda Kaul gazed at the small statue of Buddha, which her father had brought from Tibet. Raka asked many questions about her great-grandfather's adventures into Tibet and then

Both gazed at the Buddha, sole survivor of that splendour, looking as though the holocaust around him was less than the dust to him. (p.85)

However, Nanda Kaul and Raka have substantial differences: Nanda Kaul is confronted with the vacuity within herself — her indifference to the other world is born out of her dislike of the call of duty, her disgust with her past life, her role as the wife of a vice-chancellor, and her past experience of woe and suffering. Raka continues to suffer from the echoes of her tortured childhood, the endless quarrels of her parents which had left a scar on her tender sensibilities. Raka seems rather indifferent to her great-grandmother, perhaps as a result of her being a very lonesome, solitary, prematurely serious child. However, Nanda as well as Raka are human portents of isolation. Both of them need to cross the mutual barriers of communication, the obstacles in the path of affection, and both need to respond to each other's intense desire for love.

The third part of the novel narrates the story of Ila Das, who fascinates as well as repels Nanda Kaul's delicate sensibility. Ila Das, a committed social worker by profession, presents quite a contrast to Nanda Kaul. Nanda Kaul and Ila Das had been friends from childhood and their families too were closely connected. Whereas Nanda Kaul's past is filled with sadness, Ila Das's present is marked by painful events. Ila Das, faced with acute financial problems, becomes a welfare officer and is posted in the hills. She then tries to prevent an orthodox and needy villager, Preet Singh, from marrying off his seven-year-old daughter to a farmer who is a widower with seven children. Preet Singh is deeply upset. On her way to Nanda Kaul's house, Ila Das is brutally raped and murdered by Preet Singh, in an act of utter inhuman vengeance.

Nanda Kaul receives the news of this brutal act with a sense of deep shock. The police officer, P.K. Shukla, telephones Nanda Kaul to come to the police station to identify the body.

> But Nanda Kaul had ceased to listen. She had dropped the telephone. With her head still thrown back, far back, she gasped: No, no, it is a lie! No, it cannot be. It was a lie, all. She had lied to Raka, lied about everything. Her father had never been to Tibet — he had bought the little Buddha from a travelling pedlar. They had not had bears and leopards in their home, nothing but overfed dogs and bad-tempered parrots. Nor had her husband loved and cherished her and kept her like a queen — he had only done enough to keep her quiet while he carried on a lifelong affair with Miss David, the mathematics mistress, whom he had not married because she was a Christian but whom he had loved, all his life loved. And her children — the children were all alien to her nature. She neither understood nor loved them. She did not live here alone by choice — she lived here alone because that was what she was forced to do, reduced to doing. All those graces and glories with which she had tried to captivate Raka were only a fabrication: they helped

her to sleep at night, they were tranquilizers, pills. She had lied to Raka. And Ila had lied, too. Ila, too, had lied, had tried. No, she wanted to tell the man on the phone, No, she wanted to cry, but could not make a sound. Instead, it choked and swelled inside her throat. She twisted her head, then, hung it down, down, let it hang. (p.145)

Fire on Mountain thus unfolds Anita Desai's tragic vision of life, in which the innocents are made to suffer and pay a heavy price for their sincerity and innocence, as ordained by an unkind fate. The scene of the forest fire, the central symbol of the whole novel, is portrayed and repeated in many situations. Although fire is a constant danger to all those who live in a forest, it is forcefully presented in this narrative as the symbol of a grave, impending, and inevitable tragedy. Raka, overwhelmed by the sight of a copper glow, asks Nanda Kaul, "Is that the moon? Is that the full moon?" "N-no" muses Nanda Kaul. "It's a forest fire — A big fire, it seems." And she predicts that the fire will spread and the whole "village may burn in a fire that big" (p.74).

Thus, the fire on the mountain becomes a symbol of destruction and purification, the destruction of an unkind world of many Nanda Kauls and Ila Dases, of an unequal situation in which women suffer from the slings of misfortune, social inequities and injustices perpetrated on them by a cruel man-dominated world.

The montage technique projects and heightens the effect of Anita Desai's tragic vision of life. The botanical images of pine trees repeated several times signify Nanda Kaul's inner desire to merge with her natural environment. Her observation of the "yellow rose creeper" (p.17) reducing itself to a mass of grey creaks shows the process of the withering of her hopes and aspirations. Zoological images such as hens and poultry, and predatory images such as a hoopoe stabbing to death a grasshopper, only heighten the effect of man trying to enslave and vanquish his fellow men. For example, the scene of the mischievous schoolboys insulting Ila Das or the awful scene of Preet Singh pouncing upon Ila Das is a kind of human counterpart to the predatory quality of the animal world.

Just then a black shape detached itself from the jagged pile of the rock, that last rock between her and the hamlet, and sprang soundlessly at her. She staggered under its weight with a gasp that ripped through her chest. It had her by the throat. She struggled, choking, trying to stretch and stretch that gasp till it became a shout, a shout that the villagers would hear, the red dog would hear, a shout for help. But the fingers tightened. Now she tore her mouth open for breath, now she opened her eyes till they boggled, and popped, and stood out of her head as she saw, in the cold shadow, that it was Preet Singh, his lips lifted back from his teeth, his eyes blazing down at her in rage, in a passion of rage. She lifted her hands to dislodge his from her throat and she did dislodge them. They fell away, but only to tear at the cotton scarf that hung about his neck, only to wrap that about her throat, tighter, tighter, tighter, so that the last gasp rattled inside her, choked and rattled and was still. Her eyes still swivelled in their sockets, two alarmed marbles of black and white, and quickly he left the ends of the scarf, tore at her clothes, tore them off her, in long, screeching rips, till he came to her, to the dry, shrivelled, starved stick inside the wrappings, and raped her, pinned her down into the dust and the goat droppings, and raped her. Crushed back, crushed down into the earth, she lay raped, broken, still and finished. Now it was dark. (pp.142-143)

This agonizing scene of the rape and murder of Ila Das, apart from contributing to the imagistic texture of the novel, adds a new, feminist dimension to its mosaic-like form. The treatment of women — Nanda Kaul, Asha, Raka, Ila Das — highlights the mental and physical oppression to which women are subjected, and their intense suffering, loneliness and isolation are portrayed with great effect.

Images of sound and colour derived from the natural, animal and human world are significantly linked with the modes of thinking and feeling of the characters themselves. This is a significant aspect of Desai's montage-like art of fiction. For instance, Nanda Kaul in her quest for stillness and solitude shuts out the world of light and shade, sounds and voices.

> She had practised this stillness, this composure, for years, for an hour every afternoon: it was an art, not easily acquired. The most difficult had been those years in that busy house where

doors were never shut, and feet flew, or tramped, without ceasing. She remembered how she had tried to shut out sound by shutting out light, how she had spent the sleepless hour making out the direction from which a shout came, or a burst of giggles, an ominous growling from the dogs, the spray of gravel under bicycle wheels on the drive, a contest of squirrels over the guavas in the orchard, the dry rattle of eucalyptus leaves in the sun, a drop, then spray and rush of water from a tap. All was subdued, but nothing was ever still. (p.23)

These sounds invade Nanda Kaul's room and also disturb her psyche. The parrots quarrel, scream and violate Nanda Kaul's quiet world. She herself is compared to a lizard, who is shown as "imitating death".

The ambivalence between movement and stillness is a significant aspect of Anita Desai's technique. Nanda Kaul's quest for stillness was "an art, not easily acquired". She practised this art of composure an hour every day for years. This brings to mind the essence of the Hindu view of life and its basic concept of the "still point", of being a *sthitapradnya*, of the mode of seeking wisdom in stillness. This idea is also linked with the wisdom implicit in withdrawal. The desire for stillness coexists with the wish for participation in movement, and the two contrasted states of mind and activity enrich the novel.[2]

Anita Desai as an artist is deeply involved in an aesthetic mode of unfolding, of a sense of time. Novelists in modern times, as stated by David Leon Higdon, have discovered the secret of that well-known Mad Hatter in *Alice in Wonderland*. One may trace the poetics of fictional "time shapes" and discover that time, as used by modern novelists, is "amazingly malleable and elastic."[3] Time, as perceived by Nanda Kaul, in *Fire on the Mountain*, is often frozen into a still point. Time stands still. And yet, it moves backwards and forwards, kindling memories of the painful past and relating them to the ominous present. Anita Desai's art is subtle in the sense that she skilfully uses 'Process Time', 'Retrospective Time' and 'Barrier Time' in a sequential form in *Fire on the Mountain*. Process time is a kind of telescoping of the present and the future, cause and effect, choice and consequence, and this is revealed in the interaction between Nanda Kaul, Asha and Raka. Anita Desai's method of retrospective narration, especially in relation to Nanda Kaul (in chapters nineteen and twenty), leads her to the use of 'Retrospective Time', in which the narrator looks back and is transformed by the very act of looking. The forces of self and non-self, as in the case of Nanda Kaul, act and interact in moments of 'Retrospective Time'. Anita Desai also uses the fictional techniques of 'Barrier Time' in the sense that she breaks off one end of the time line, and inserts it as a 'barrier moment' which reveals the psyche of the character. This is carefully achieved by unfolding Nanda Kaul's earlier and later phases of life, as well as the initial and the later phases of Ila Das. The 'Barrier Time' is a structural device for delving deep into the psychic state of the characters and projecting their point of view and their vision. Anita Desai's use of these three time devices is extremely subtle and forms part of her carefully achieved pattern.

The 'time dimension' implicit in the interaction between stillness and movement is indeed a significant aspect of the montage-like technique and vision of Anita Desai in *Fire on the Mountain*.

NOTES

1. Anita Desai, *Fire on the Mountain* (New Delhi: Allied Publishers, 1977), p.3. All subsequent references are to this edition.

2. Various aspects of Anita Desai's art of fiction have been discussed and commented upon perceptively by a number of critics such as Madhusudan Prasad, *Anita Desai the Novelist* (Allahabad, 1981); R.S. Sharma, *Anita Desai* (New Delhi, 1981); Malashri Lal, 'Anita Desai: *Fire on the Mountain*' in *Major Indian Novels*, ed. N.S. Pradhan (New Delhi, 1985); Prema Nandakumar, 'Sombre the Shadows and Sudden the Nights: A Study of Anita Desai's Novels' in *Perspectives on Indian Fiction in English*, ed. M.K.Naik (New Delhi, 1985). In addition, reviews of her novels have appeared in various journals.

3. David Leon Higdon, *Time and English Fiction* (London: Macmillan, 1977), p.1.

VRINDA NABAR

The four-dimensional reality: Anita Desai's *Clear Light of Day*

Readers commonly respond to *Clear Light of Day*[1] with misgivings about what they call "its real Indianness". According to them, (a) its ethos is too Westernized; (b) Bim is not "typically Indian"; (c) the *koels* at the beginning of the novel, like the other Indian images in it, are too strident to be more than obvious attempts at introducing local colour.

These doubts could equally appropriately be applied to the study of Desai's fiction as a whole. They are partly related to the Indianness or alleged lack of it in Anita Desai's work. More precisely, however, they are responses to the very select section of Indian society which she writes about. It is, obviously, a largely Westernized section. But Westernization, as seen in the novels, is a definite aspect of urban Indian reality.

It should be said of Anita Desai that she presents this aspect more convincingly, more authentically too, than any other contemporary Indian English writer of fiction. The authenticity is strengthened by the fact that she is also the most skilled of the Indian English novelists from the point of view of pure craftsmanship. Whatever one's differences with her in terms of attitudes/stances taken in the novels, it cannot in all fairness be denied that her work is characterized by her awareness of the formal needs of the novel as a genre. Nor are these aspects of the novel used as mere appurtenances. They are intrinsic to the story and are handled with an instinctive and imaginative understanding of their potential in fiction.

This is clearly seen in the present novel. Anita Desai is reported to have described it as an attempt to write "a four-dimensional piece on how a family's life moves backwards and forwards in a period of time".[2] The fourth dimension, she has further clarified, is the dimension of Time.[3] The novel is in four chapters, effectively four parts. Each of these deals with distinct periods in the lives of the principal characters, the first and the last chapters being set in the present.

The "four-dimensional" reality is used by Desai to make the intervening sections more than just a conventional trip down memory lane. While she retains control of the narrative, the scenes from the past are made to relate unmistakably to the present consciousness of the characters. Tara's homecoming triggers off in Bim memories of a past that has lost much of its enchantment in the drab framework of the present. The past is suppressed by Bim in an attempt to put the lid on unpleasant pointers to the truth about her situation. At the beginning of the novel, we see her largely in relation to the myth she has allowed to develop around her. In chapter four, Tara wonders how this myth had grown, seeing little to support it in the Bim she now encounters:

> She had always thought Bim so competent, so capable. Everyone had thought that — Aunt Mira, the teachers at school, even Raja. But Bim seemed to stampede through the house like a dishevelled storm, creating more havoc than order. Tara would be ashamed to run a house like this. Bakul would have been horrified if she did. Then how had Bim acquired her fine reputation? Or had her old capability, her old competence begun to crumble now and go to seed? Tara saw how little she had really observed — either as a child or as a grown woman. (p.148)

Tara's return home, her tactless blundering into the past, her naive responses to the present, force Bim to face up to the real emptiness of her life. It is not as if she was actually unaware of it, merely that she had tried to suppress the awareness. The journey into the past could thus be seen as a journey into the subconscious. Desai gives it just that degree of distortion, of formlessness, while adhering to the sequential pattern, to create the impression of a "psycho-analytic" process at work. Tara's presence and the undercurrents she generates form a kind of figurative psychiatrist's couch on which Bim finds herself, as it were.

Just before Bim comes to terms with her real situation, she is shown as dangerously close to neurosis. Tara says she talks to herself. Almost paranoid, Bim begins to see Tara as a mean, prying person. She resents the unspoken opinion that spinsterhood was making her queer. When her anger erupts, it finds an easy target in Baba, whom she has never consciously admitted as a brake on her freedom to choose.

Bim's loss of control is followed by a mood of introspection in which she sees "as well as by the clear light of day" that she is inextricably bound to her siblings, as dependent on their love and approval as they are on hers. Whether such a denouement is wholly satisfying or not, the direction it takes is significant for two reasons. First, it gives us evidence of an organic growth in character. Bim, like most of Desai's other characters, is not the "same" at the end of the novel. Desai uses the various events, incidents, etc. in the plot to affect her characters substantially. In this way she prevents the characters from becoming static and the novel from degenerating into little more than an anecdotal narrative. Secondly, the kind of reconciliation with the self that Bim achieves, inseparable as it is from her family set-up, emphasizes that *Clear Light of Day* cannot be anything other than an "Indian" novel. This is not merely because it is set in Delhi, or because its characters are all Indian, but because its situations, images, as well as its central conflicts can be satisfactorily explained only in an Indian context.

Bim's entire dilemma is born out of this context. Approaching middle age, Bim is fairly representative of a certain type of contemporary Indian urban woman — single, independent, self-assured. At a superficial level, such a woman may be seen as "Westernized". After all, Bim even smokes!

Further, she clearly belongs to a class easily identifiable in Desai's novels, a class which is comfortably off, Anglicized, even neo-colonial. However, like Desai's other female characters, like most of the Indian women whom she recognizably resembles, Bim is also conditioned by her Indian environment. It is *this* environment which positions her as the moral and physical caretaker of the Das household after her parents die. Their deaths unhinge timid Mira *masi* who had functioned capably enough as long as they pulled the strings and gave the orders. As she disintegrates into alcoholism, Tara marries

Bakul, largely to "escape", as she admits later. Bim, saddled with her alcoholic aunt and retarded brother, accommodates them in her scheme of things. Her Western counterpart in similar circumstances would have most likely dumped them both in appropriate homes in order to preserve her existential freedom. Even Raja leaves for Hyderabad as soon as he is physically fit enough to do so.

Bim's continued solitude is likewise a reflection of her environment. Except for the unfortunate trespasses of Dr. Biswas, she remains singularly devoid of any male companionship. Nor does this singleness appear to produce any visible tensions or conflicts. In another, Western, context it is easy to imagine Bim having some kind of a compulsive relationship with a man — sexual, of course, even if not necessarily harmonious or secure — if only as an emotional release.

The Das household, seen at different periods of time, follows a recognizable pattern. The endless game of bridge the parents play, punctuated by their visits to the Club, the self-contained world in which they move, throw the children closer together. Raja is the characteristic older son, spoilt, self-centred, largely irresponsible. Tara, timid and insecure, generally withdrawn from the games Bim and Raja play, draws comfort and warmth from the presence of Mira *masi*. Mira *masi* is true to type, a widowed aunt, a financial dependant and therefore *persona non grata* in the household. At the same time, she provides the only affection and caring the children know. Desai effectively sums up her presence as associated, for Tara, with her smell:

> she was solid as a bed, she smelt of cooking and was made of knitting. Tara could wrap herself up in her as in an old soft shawl. This Tara needed for she had lost most at Baba's birth and the turning of the entire family from her to the new baby. Wrapped in the folds of Aunt Mira's white cotton sari, or into her loosely knitted grey shawl, or the plump billows of the plum-coloured quilt in winter, she became baby again, breathing in her aunt's smell, finding in it a deep musty comfort. (p.109)

In the Indian context, Ms. Desai could not have picked a more effective image. The role of an elderly aunt or an *ayah* as the children's most constant companion was and is an all-too-familiar feature of Indian family life. This presence is usually bound up with a sense of the person's smell. In later years, it is this smell that remains as a memory, not so much the way a person looked or dressed.

Having "escaped" from home, the two siblings are not wholly "free". Guilt becomes a major emotion in the novel. While there is nothing specifically Indian about such guilt it supports the basic ambience of Indianness. Faced with Raja's letter in the first chapter the reader responds principally to its insensitive tone. In chapter three, the letter, seen retrospectively, becomes a symbol of Raja's sense of guilt. That guilt is evident at the end of chapter two when Raja leaves, promising to return and look after Bim and Baba. It is evident in his angry justification of his action, provoked by Bim's silence which is more effective than any reproof:

> She kept calm while Raja packed his bags, put away all his things, telling her that now he would go to Hyderabad. Looking up at her as she watched silently, he shouted 'I have to go. Now I can go. I have to begin my life some time, don't I? You don't want me to spend all my life down in this hole, do you? You don't think I can go on living just to keep my brother and sister company, do you?'
>
> 'I never said a word', said Bim coldly.
>
> 'You don't have to. It's written all over your face. Just go, go, take your face away. Don't sit there staring. Don't stop me.'
> (pp.100-101)

Had Bim reacted otherwise, a bitter confrontation might have provided Raja with a framework to rationalize his departure. When he goes, he is unable to help himself but he continues to feel uneasy about this assertion of his choice. His letter is a means to prove to Bim that he still cares for her, that he wishes to help. It is characteristic of his ego-ridden temperament that he can only make reparations in this clumsly, hurtful way.

Tara's marriage, seen as an escape, liberates her in several superficial ways. When she returns she is socially poised, more confident, less nervous. Yet, coming back, she slips into the old grooves in a manner which irritates her pompous diplomat husband. He can't understand her wanting to spend time with her sister and brother instead of romping around New Delhi with him. The reason for Tara's confused inertia is that her homecoming shows her sharply and unmistakably what she had left Bim to cope with.

As Tara reluctantly confronts the reality of life in her childhood home, Desai uses an incident from adolescence as a symbol of her guilt. As young girls, Bim and Tara had accompanied some neighbours on a picnic to the Lodhi Gardens. Bim had been attacked by a swarm of bees. Tara recalls abandoning Bim and fleeing away to the others — to safety. Bim's matter-of-fact explanation — Tara had to get help — is not acceptable to Tara. She continues to beat her breast, metaphorically speaking, at having escaped and abandoned Bim. It is easy to see a parallel between this somewhat superficial incident and the real abandoning of Bim by her sister and brother.

Like Raja and Tara, Bim too is subject to a kind of guilt. At one level it is apparent that her staying back was a matter of compulsion, not of choice. At another level, however, one suspects that, even given the choice, Bim would have found it extremely difficult to go away voluntarily as Raja and Tara had done. Having stayed, however, she sees her action as a kind of sacrifice. Naturally, too, she feels hemmed-in. A sort of defensive mechanism makes her project herself as self-sufficient and satisfied with her mode of living. This is why her attack on Baba produces the turmoil in her. It makes her guilt surface, and forces her to recognize the ambivalent feelings in herself.

The handling of these characters makes it apparent that an exclusive concentration on the narrow boundaries of class-experience need not in itself be limiting. It becomes so only if the writer allows such exclusion to become a fetish. And Desai appears dangerously close to doing so. Her novels, understandably, deal with the class she knows best, but they do so at the expense of shutting out the much more complex Indian reality. She admits as much in reply to Ramesh Srivastava's observation that vast areas of the Indian experience cannot be within her easy reach: "Lack of experience may be a handicap but lack of sensitivity, thought, intelligence or memory would be far greater ones. I do restrict myself to writing about people and situations I know or can understand."[4]

In the novels such a stand tends to black out the kind of intermingling of classes which is inevitable in the Indian context. Where presented, the method is far from satisfactory. Its limitations can be seen in the depiction of servants who are commonly described as being either sullen and inefficient (like Janaki) or cringing and false (like Bhakta, Hyder Ali's driver). At a more serious level, such exclusion raises doubts about the creative development of a writer. It is, after all, a writer's business to expand his or her experience, not to justify a fictional ivory tower based on a limited class-experience. The drawbacks in Ms. Desai's refusal to transcend her class-conditioning are apparent in at least two major instances in this novel, both of which affect the authenticity of the Indian experience.

The first relates to Mira *masi*. We have already noted how Ms. Desai brings out the essence of Mira *masi*'s presence — her smell. It must be added that this picture, though convincing, is still somewhat amorphous since it does not really individualize Mira *masi*, but merely puts her into a recognizable slot. All the same it emerges as authentic, especially in contrast to the attempt to shade in Mira *masi*'s past, obviously done in order to give her depth:

> Aunt Mira was younger than their mother although she looked so much older. She had been twelve years old when she married and was a virgin when she was widowed — her young student husband, having left to study in England immediately after their wedding, caught a cold in the rain one winter night, and died. She was left stranded with his family and they blamed her bitterly for his death; it was her unfortunate horoscope that had brought it about, they said. She should be made to pay for her guilt. Guiltily, she scrubbed and washed and cooked for them. At night she massaged her mother-in-law's legs and nursed wakeful babies and stitched trousseaux for her sister-in-law. Of course she aged. Not only was her hair white but she was nearly bald. At least that saved her from being used by her brothers-in-law who would have put the widow to a different use had she been more appetising. Since she was not, they eyed her unpleasing person sullenly and made jokes loudly enough for her to overhear. There was laughter, still they grew bored. She stayed with them so long that she became boring. They suspected her of being a parasite. It was time she was turned out. She was turned out. Another household could find some use for her; cracked pot, torn rag, picked bone. (p.108)

That is Mira *masi*'s history, dismissed in just one paragraph. The details are Indian alright, but too pat. They sound suspect, a little too reeled-off. They almost add up to The Life of the Typical Indian Widow. One might argue that Mira *masi* was too lifeless to be individualized in any distinctive way, but such a view does not support the evidence of the final drama — her alcoholism and insanity, both consequent upon the death of Bim's parents.

As a psychological outcome of these deaths, Mira *masi*'s collapse is an example of imaginative versatility. But Ms. Desai flounders because the imaginative world, not sustained by the reality of experience, produces weird pictures of Mira *masi*'s madness. She projects an Ophelia-like lewdness and this sense of her is borne out by Bim's own recollection of her aunt as a drowned Ophelia. While the form Ophelia's 'madness takes is logically accountable within the dramatic framework of *Hamlet* there are no corresponding logical connections in the instance of Mira *masi*. In her the transformation from self-effacing aunt to dipsomaniac slattern comes across as bizarre and inappropriate, an unhappy consequence thrust upon her by the novelist.

Almost as ludicrous is the description of the Misra household in chapter three. In it, the Misras are contrasted with the Das household to the partial detriment of the latter. There is an ironic reference to the paraphernalia which constituted the hallmark of respectability to Tara's parents: "curtains at the windows, carpets on the floors, solid pieces of furniture placed at regular intervals, plates that matched each other on the table, white uniforms for the house servants."

The Misras are meant to provide a healthy contrast, but even so a fastidious reserve on the novelist's part converts informality into sloppiness and chaos. The picture painted is moreover so inaccurate in parts as to underscore the writer's remoteness from her subject. For instance we are told that "meals were ordered in a haphazard way and when the family smelt something good cooking, they dipped impatiently into the cooking pots as soon as it was ready instead of waiting for the clock hands to move to the appointed hour."

One can't really conceive of a conventional Indian household operating in this way. The plates may not match, the servants stay barechested, the furniture appears irregular and unfashionable, but routine there most certainly will be. It will, besides, be a routine that will not permit of whimsical dipping into cooking-pots since, to the traditional Hindu, such an act would make the food "unclean."

But even these cameos are not only wholly unacceptable. They may appear partly limited but a basic sense of wanting to do the right thing is apparent. Not so when certain other experiences are presented. In this novel, the most obvious example is the tea party at the Biswases'. Before it, we see Dr. Biswas, an earnest, pathetic figure whose love of Mozart is a subject of immense amusement to Raja and Bim. Already an attitude which becomes obtrusively neo-colonial is beginning to assert itself. Not being "one of us," Dr. Biswas has, of course, no right to admire Mozart. In response to the knowledge that he does, Raja can only clutch at his heart and theatrically murmur, "Ach so Mozart!"

One might concede here that it is Raja and Bim whose responses are depicted, that the novelist may be using them to show us an aspect of Indian life which is real if not desirable — the existence of the brown sahib and memsahib. It is less easy to approach the tea party in a similar manner:

> The tea party was of course a mistake and Bim scowled and cursed herself for having softened and let herself in for what was a humiliation and a disaster for everyone concerned.
>
> Had Mrs Biswas dressed for it? Bim had never seen anyone so dressed. So bathed, so powdered, she seemed to be dusted all over with flour. Perhaps she had fallen into a flour bin, like a large bun. But she smelt so powerfully of synthetic flowers, it must be powder after all. And her white sari crackled with starch, like a biscuit. And her hair gleamed with coconut oil, and flakes of gold glinted at the lobes of her ears and in the ringed folds of her neck. Altogether a piece of confectionery, thought Bim.
>
> She was given a platter with all the goodies already heaped on it — neatly counted out, so many biscuits, so many pieces of mithai, so many fritters and a spoonful of chutney. Similar plates with exactly the same number of goodies were handed to Dr. Biswas, one kept by her. They ate.
>
> A china cabinet against the wall watched them. It stood on four legs and housed little plaster figures from Germany — a miniature beer mug, Hansel and Gretel skipping in a meadow, a squirrel dressed in a daisy chain. There were Indian dolls, less travelled but more worn, tinsel garlands flaking off onto red or-

gandie saris and gold turbans. There were clay toys in cane baskets — yellow bananas, green chillies. A parrot. A cow. A plastic baby. And they all stared at Bim munching her way through the goodies. Dr. Biswas stared at his brown shoes, so highly polished. He ate nothing. (pp. 90-91)

Sniggers and loud laughter have been, in my experience, the commonest responses to this passage. One needs to examine these responses, to try to understand what provokes them. Essentially, what is being depicted is a middle-class drawing-room which is more representative of urban India than the Das household could ever be. Mrs. Biswas, powdered and bedecked with jewellery, is likewise a "typical" middle-class Indian housewife. The plate of goodies, the china cabinet with its odd mixture of curios, its plastic baby and clay fruit, are similarly redolent of middle-class India. What moves us to laughter is the slight distortion in context which makes all these images obvious objects of satire.

The tea party is to prove decisively the incompatibility of Dr. Biswas and Bim as marriage partners. Further, it will do so in a way which somehow discredits Dr. Biswas rather than Bim. As Bim scurries away she significantly notes: "How much his mother's son he was... he had inherited her gift for loading the weight of his self-sacrifices onto others." It is with conscious design that Dr. Biswas and his mother are presented in an unattractive comical light and there is no evidence to support the stand that it is Bim alone who looks at them in this way. On the contrary, the novelist appears a firm ally, since our response is to the mother and son comedy rather than to any irony in the depiction of Bim's reactions.

A neo-colonial attitude is at work here,[5] a class-consciousness which is sufficiently present in the Indian context to become recognizable as an upper middle-class characteristic. It is neo-colonial because it is a take-on, a caricature, of the old colonial stance which was convinced of the superiority of its own lifestyle and mocked attempts by the natives to "ape" the manners of the masters. Such class superiority is blatantly evident in urban India. It is unfortunate that Anita Desai herself is not always above a supercilious wrinkling of the nostrils when she is on such territory.

NOTES

1. Anita Desai, *Clear Light of Day* (New Delhi: Allied Publishers, 1980). All subsequent references are to this edition.

2. In an interview with Sunil Sethi. Rāmesh Srivastava refers to this interview in 'Anita Desai at Work', *Perspectives on Anita Desai*, ed. Ramesh Srivastava, (Ghaziabad: Vimal Prakashan, 1984).

3. Ibid.

4. Ibid.

5. I use the phrase "neo-colonial" in the absence of one which best approximates the stance taken.

O P MATHUR

A metaphor of reality: A study of the protagonist of *Midnight's Children*

William Walsh rightly points out that the "huge purpose" of Salman Rushdie's *Midnight's Children*[1] is "the personification and realisation of Indian life."[2] The novel is a piece of faction by one born in India but settled abroad who tries to re-create his homeland, mixing memory and desire, fact and fantasy, reality and vision, time and timelessness. Rushdie suggestively remarks:

> And one such suspicious generalisation may be that writers in my position, exiles or emigrants or expatriates, are haunted by some sense of loss, some urge to reclaim, to look back, even at the risk of being mutated into pillars of salt. But if we do look back, we must also do so in the knowledge — which gives rise to profound uncertainties — that our physical alienation from India almost inevitably means that we will not be capable of reclaiming precisely the thing that was lost; that we will, in short, create fictions, not actual cities or villages, but invisible ones, imaginary homelands, Indias of the mind.[3]

In *Midnight's Children* this imaginary truth is conveyed through a complex strategy, the centre of which is the narrator-protagonist Saleem Sinai who is the embodiment of a supreme moment of history, a crystallization of an evolving mood, a distillation of a vision, nostalgic, critical and philosophical. He is a camera eye, which is itself cracked and fragmented, with, as the novelist remarks, some of its fragments missing. But in spite of it, or perhaps because of it, he is able to project what may be called a sort of prismatic vision of reality, partial, fissured and fragmented, but highly absorbing and deeply meaningful. Afraid of absurdity, he is frantically engaged in a quest for meaning (p.4), thus personifying what he calls "a very Indian lust for allegory" (p.110).

Saleem Sinai is one of the "midnight's children," born between 12 midnight and 1 A.M. on the night of August 14-15, 1947, the hour of the nascence of free India. Out of a total of 1,001 such children, 420 die and 581 survive up to 1957. All these imaginary beings meet and discuss and quarrel in the parliament of Saleem's mind, forming a Midnight's Children's Conference. These children, a sort of multi-headed monster speaking in the myriad tongues of Babel, are a metaphor for Indian society, "the very essence of multiplicity" (p.274), one thousand and one ways of looking at things.

> I found children from Maharashtra loathing Gujaratis, and fair-skinned northerners reviling Dravidian "Blackies"; there were religious rivalries; and class entered our councils. The rich children turned up their noses at being in such lowly company; the Brahmins began to feel uneasy at permitting even their thoughts to touch the thoughts of untouchables; while, among the low-born, the pressures of poverty and Communism were becoming evident... (p.206)

They represent the nation's psyche:

> Midnight's children can be made to represent many things, according to your point of view; they can be seen as the last throw of everything antiquated and retrogressive in our myth-ridden nation, whose defeat was entirely desirable in the context of a modernizing, twentieth-century economy; or as the true hope of freedom, which is now forever extinguished, but what they must not become is the bizarre creation of a rambling, diseased mind. (p.240)

All these children have special gifts or powers or physical peculiarities. Two of them, Saleem and Shiva, born exactly at the stroke of midnight, have remarkable complementary gifts — nose and knees. The destructive Shiva blessed with powerful knees has "the gifts of war" while Saleem has "the greatest talent of all — the ability to look into the hearts and minds of men" (p.239). His long beaked nose is a symbol of this power to observe reality, the "smell" of it as it were — which a denizen of the "old world" thinks performs the function of a stethoscope (p.17). The confusion is appropriate, for is it not with his nose, with his "nasal ethics" (p.380) that Saleem explores the state of the nation? But this is to anticipate.

Having been born at a crucial moment of history, Saleem claims "a place at the centre of things" (p.288), and, on the authority of Prime Minister Nehru's letter to him, "the role of the mirror-of-the-nation more than the sloganized centrality of Indira Gandhi" (p.510). In surprisingly numerous ways, India is Saleem Sinai and Saleem Sinai is India. The very time of his "clock-ridden, crime-stained birth" (p.4) handcuffs him to Indian history. Geography too is no less important. Sinai is a small triangular peninsula with associations of "the-place-of-revelation, of put-off-thy shoes, of commandments and golden calves" (p.365) — in short, something like India in miniature. Saleem Sinai's "map face" also represents the map of India, her vastness reflected in its largeness (p.144). The disfiguring "birth-marks" on the face seem to be a creation of the holocaust of Partition. The bulbous "Byzantine domes" of the temples may be suggestive of the Himalayas just as the "ice-like eccentricity" of his "sky-blue eyes" (p.145) seems to point to the azure skies of Kashmir. The "dark stains" spread down the "western hairline" and the "dark patch" colouring the "eastern ear" clearly stand for the two wings of Pakistan, and the "something lacking in the chin" (p.144) might be a hint at the thinness of the southern part of the Indian peninsula. Saleem's long nose, the most marked feature of his physiognomy, appears to be indicative of India's pride and self-glorification which makes Indians so valuable that Saleem's nose ran (p.145). At the time of the Chinese aggression, "while the nation puffed itself up", Saleem's "sinuses also puffed up" (p.359), and when Indians attacked the Chinese his nasal passages too were in "a state of acute crisis" (p.360). His highly sensitive olfactory powers have both physical and moral dimensions, for he classifies smells by colour, weight, geometric system and morality, "the science of nasal ethics":

> Sacred: purdah-veils, halal meat, muezzin's towers, prayer-mats; profane: Western records, pig meat, alcohol. (p.380)

Again in Bangladesh:

> In the midst of the rubble of war, I discovered fair-and-unfair. Unfairness smelled like onions, the sharpness of its perfume brought tears to my eyes. Seized by the bitter aroma of injustice... I smelled her traitress's smile. (pp. 442-43)

Certain other physical features of Saleem are also quite significant. For some time after his birth he does not blink. The "immobility" of his eyelids seems to suggest a steady gaze at the fleeting phenomena of this material world, the timelessness of the vision of Indian seers. Saleem's "literally disintegrating" and "fissured" body from which history pours out is a possible reference to the underlying political fragmentation and divisive tendencies of Indian politics, past and present, which have contributed to the making of its history. In fact, fragmentation, the bane of Indian society and politics, runs through the theme and technique of the novel. Moreover, his "white" father (having lost the pigment of his skin on account of disease) and his "ebony mother" may be indicative of the East-West confluence in the society and culture of resurgent India. In another respect too Saleem acquires a multiple representative role. By the revengeful baby-swapping of the nurse Mary Pareira, Saleem, really the son of a poor man, is transferred to a rich family and Shiva takes his place. But then how did he acquire the famous family nose? There seems to be a merger of identities in a shared Indian dream:

> In fact, all over the new India, the dream we all shared, children were being born who were only partially the offspring of their parents — the children of midnight were also the children of *the time*: fathered, you understand by history. It can happen. Especially in a country which is itself a sort of dream. (p.137)

Saleem's representative quality thus transcends the historical and the geographical into the cultural and the philosophical.

Saleem's growth also mirrors the development of free India. His launching upon "an heroic program of self-enlargement" (p.145) soon after his birth and his huge appetite seem to be a pointer to India's ambitious five-year plans and the large amounts of foreign aid, especially American (mark the American spelling of "program"), swallowed by them. Saleem bears "the burden of history" (p.457) throughout his life. The events leading to the imposition of Emergency also find a mirror in his life. The labour pains of his wife Parvati-Laylah begin on June 12, 1975, when Justice Jag Mohan Lal Sinha delivers his famous judgement against Indira Gandhi, who also is in the process of "giving birth to a child of her own" (p.499). Parvati's son arrives at the precise moment of the birth of the Emergency which, indeed, the new-born child personifies. He has large ears but is dumb and does not even whimper (p.501), and his eyes also soon grow to be as large as saucers and his face as serious as the grave (p.527) — in brief, an image of the censorship-ridden, sad and reflective, but inquisitive, mood of the Emergency:

> We, the children of Independence, rushed wildly and too fast into our future: he, Emergency-born, will be, is already more cautious, biding his time; but when he acts, he will be impossible to resist. Already, he is stronger, harder, more resolute than I: when he sleeps, his eyeballs are immobile beneath their lids. Aadam Sinai, child of knees-and-nose, does not (as far as I can tell) surrender to dreams. (p.507)

Saleem's life covers the period from Independence to the lifting of the Emergency, but charming spots of bygone times are also visible through the "open sesame" of the perforated bedsheet. The gamut of events covered by the novel include the agitation against the Rowlatt Bill, the Jalianwalla Bagh massacre, the formation of the Indian National Army, the dropping of the atom bombs on Japan, communal riots, the dawn of Independence, the assassination of Mahatma Gandhi, the Hindu Succession Act, the closing of the Suez Canal, the submission of the report of the States Reorganization Commission, language riots, the elections of 1957 and 1962, the Chinese aggression, the Nanavati case, the theft of Hazrat Bal, the liberation of Goa, the death of Nehru, the Kutch war and the Indo-Pakistan war of 1965, the Bangladesh war, and the imposition and the lifting of Emergency. On account of Saleem's stay in Pakistan, some events of that country have also been brought into focus — the rise of Ayub to power, the formation of a Combined Opposition Party, the farce of the elections, the assumption of the Presidency by Yahya Khan, the elections of 1970, and the repression let loose upon the eastern wing and its struggle for independence. The novelist has narrated, commented upon or referred to these events and their varied real or imaginary relationship with the narrator, his family and the 'midnight's children'. He has also portrayed the feel of those times through the fertile but rambling imagination and the fractured and fragmented but meaningful vision of an ironical narrator with a representatively multiple identity.

Saleem is linked to history by different "modes of connection" — "actively-literally, passively-metaphorically, actively-metaphorically and passively-literally" (p.285-86), which he goes on to analyze and illustrate. Saleem stands in manifold relationships to history — as its twin-companion, its creator and its victim, in addition to being a chronicler, a participant, an ironic overviewer and an inspired visionary. The date of his birth itself is a dividing line between the old world and the new. The vignettes of the past, especially the personality of Tai the boatman and the episode of love arising through the medium of a perforated bedsheet articulate the author's nostalgia for the past which embodied sterling qualities like simplicity, sincerity, love, attachment to the soil and a cosmopolitan code of values which are timeless. As the boatman Tai who not only claims to have seen Jesus Christ on his supposed visit to Kashmir but also to have transcended time and history says: "I have watched the mountains being born; I have seen emperors die" (p.11). He himself is shot, standing between the Indian and the Pakistani armies fighting over Kashmir. The personality of Tai provides a symbol, an ethical framework for the subsequent periods of strife, bloodshed and fragmentation. Saleem is a humanist at heart who dislikes the walls that divide mankind into fragments and hates everything that suffocates the free spirit of man. His ideal appears to be Tai the boatman, the timeless being, who embodies a triply idyllic charm of the old world, of the beautiful nature of Kashmir and of the freedom and essential unity of mankind. Another such character is Mian Abdullah 'the Hummingbird', an active opponent of Partition, whose joyful ecstasy in work is symbolized by his constant humming and who also falls a victim to the knives of Muslim fanatics. With Tai-Abdullah as his model, the narrator views the scenario of history with pungent irony. He seems to join the Boatman and the Hummingbird in a trinity of Tai-Abdullah-Saleem.

The narrator's moral stance is noticeable in the large number of descriptions or even passing references to historical men and events. He is an inveterate hater of fanaticism and communalism. In fact, his mother announces her pregnancy to save the life of one Lifafa Das from Muslim communalists (p.86). He dislikes the Partition (pp.89-90), presents his father as having a distrust for Jinnah (p.94) and impatiently condemns the language riots in Bombay (pp.225 ff.). Many such references are witty and light-hearted, but the targets at which laughter is directed reveal the teller. The narrator's ire is really aroused by the Emergency which "damaged reality so badly that nobody ever managed to put it together again" (p.500). His son, Aadam Aziz, who was born at the precise moment of the declaration of Emergency falls ill of a "darkly metaphorical" illness which Saleem feels will be cured only when the Emergency is over. He imagines the children of the midnight of Emergency being "Test- and hysterectomized", denied the possibility of reproducing themselves (p.523). With this, the hope that was generated at the moment of Independence was also drained. The narrator has a word for it — "Sperectomy: the draining out of hope" (p.521).

An important fact of the narrator's comments on the Emergency is his dislike of "cocksure men and women." In spite of his large flapping ears like those of the elephant-headed god Ganesh with which he presumably gathers much information, Aadam Aziz determinedly refuses to utter a sound, and even when a green medicinal powder is given to him his cheeks become puffed up with his resolution not to let any sound escape. This disease vanishes with the lifting of the Emergency.

The traumatic experiences seem to have brought about a profound change in the narrator. The lifting of the Emergency leaves him dazed but unenthusiastic:

> The Janata Party ... did not seem to me (when I heard about it) to represent a new dawn; but may be I'd managed to cure myself of the optimism virus at last — may be others, with the disease still in their blood, felt otherwise. At any rate, I've had — I had had, on that March day — enough, more than enough, of politics. (p.525)

One who began his life with the hands of the clock joining in respectful greeting, full of gusto and optimism, has now reached a stage of desperation, "cracking now, fission of Saleem... only a broken creature spilling pieces of itself into the street" (p.552). This change is the most telling commentary on the period of the first thirty years or so of independent India, and the frustrations and disillusionments created by it.

Though Rushdie has in another novel fantasized about Pakistan, it would not be out of place to point to his portrait of that land of the pure, "that, God-ridden country" (p.350) in the present novel. Even as a boy of eleven he is suspicious of the army and has only one word for the seizure of power by Ayub — "treason" (p.348). He plays at making revolutions on the dinner table, shifting salt-cellars and bowls of chutney (p.348). Though he is in Pakistan, his personality is attuned to stable India: "the *status quo* was preserved in India; in my life, nothing changed either" (p.351). The conditions in Pakistan stir his very being and he is forced to pronounce a direct value judgement, something very unusual for the narrator:

> in a country where the truth is what it is instructed to be, reality quite literally ceases to exist so that everything becomes possible except what we are told is the case; and may be this was the difference between my Indian childhood and Pakistani adolescence — that in the first I was beset by an infinity of alternative realities, while in the second I was adrift, disorientated, amid an equally infinite number of falsenesses, unrealities and lies (p.389).

In fact, there is something of loneliness in the personality and career of the picaresque hero Saleem Sinai — Saleem, the straightforward, lost in the desert of Sinai: "but when all that is said and done; it is the name of the desert — of barrenness, infertility, dust; the name of the end" (p.365). He does not seem to lack an identity: it is only that multiple identities press upon him — a mirror of the fragmentation and multiplicity of Indian society and the confusion of social, religious, regional and parochial identities under which Indians suffer. Sometimes they even forget that they are Indians, just as Saleem forgets his name and is reminded of it only after the victory in Bangladesh. Saleem also represents the intellectual, imaginative Indian who can think, feel and communicate with others, whose mind is a parliament of various viewpoints. In addition to being a keen observer, he is also gifted with the rare quality of irony even at his own expense. The novel is full of fantastic ironies and ironical fantasies. But Saleem is no cynic. He is deeply interested in life and in the men and women around him. He loves life and freedom and ridicules whatever is outdated, narrow and constricting. Though a Muslim, he mocks at the paraphernalia of prayer and sympathizes with his grandfather's decision not to pray, "unable to worship a God in whose existence he could not wholly disbelieve" (p.6). He makes fun of the institution of 'purdah' in the episode of the perforated bedsheet and has an appreciation for the courage of his grandmother's unorthodox decision to take up the gemstone business while his grandfather sits "hidden behind the veil which the stroke had dropped over his brain " (p.7). The hatred of narrow communalism is in his family, for his grandfather threw out a tutor who taught bigotry and hatred to his children. The grandfather stood by his decision even to the point of starving.

The sacrifice of Tai the boatman and of Abdullah the Hummingbird for communal harmony and brotherhood have already been discussed. In fact, the superficial objectivity of narrative perspective and the sharp radiant ironies are woven from the threads of sincerity and love which encompass the whole of mankind. The protagonist emerges as an Indian at the crossroads of history, gifted with a fertile imagination, having no illusions and mental cobwebs, and cherishing truth, sincerity, love and tolerance even admidst a barren and hostile world. Disenchanted, he can laugh at himself as well as at others. There are not many direct value judgements, but the highest values underlie the whole narration which may be said to be an examination of the contemporary against the perspective of the eternal and the universal embodied in the wisdom and mythologies of various lands.

Saleem Sinai, with all his humanism, talents and inadequacies, is an individual worthy of admiration, sympathy and love, a paradigm of an alienated human soul "sucked into the annihilating whirlpool of the multitudes, and unable to live or die in peace" (p. 552); and also a provoking metaphor for the contemporary fragmented Indian reality and a unified philosophical vision enveloping it: "to understand me, you'll have to swallow a world" (p.458). The narrator is not a "lucid reflector" but a bizarre refractor of reality and he helps us towards a better understanding of contemporary society and of historical events, figures and trends by interpreting them from a supremely comic angle based on a stance which is profoundly moral, humane and cosmopolitan.

NOTES

1. Salman Rushdie, *Midnight's Children* (New York: Avon Books, 1982). All subsequent references are to this edition. (The book was first published in 1980.)

2. William Walsh, 'India and the Novel', in *The New Pelican Guide to English Literature*, ed. Boris Ford (Harmondsworth: Penguin Books, 1983), Vol.8, p.257.

3. Salman Rushdie, 'Reclaiming a City and a History', *Express Magazine (The Indian Express*, March 11, 1984), p.5.

VINEY KIRPAL

The perfect bubble: A study of Anita Desai's *In Custody*

Calcutta, in Anita Desai's *Voices in the City*,[1] is easily recognizable as the crowded metropolis and busy port city of West Bengal. Situated on the Hooghly and skirting the Bay of Bengal, it appears in the novel with its familiar landmarks and characteristics — the Howrah bridge, the swarming crowds, the trams thundering past, the hubbub of commerce, the small, painted boats of *lungi*-clad fishermen, the neon and naphtha lights, the coffee houses (haunts of the city's intellectuals) and so on.

Mirpore in Desai's *In Custody*,[2] is not like Calcutta in *Voices in the City*. Mirpore is unidentifiable as a particular city on the map of India and yet it is every Indian city. It is not imaged to build a background or a scene which has a locale-bound quality, but is more in the allusive strain and is brought in to evoke an image of contemporary India. Beneath the apparently loose lumping together of protean detail, it is really a concentrated imaging, like long shots of a camera directing its full gaze upon the different parts needed to put together the mosaic whole. It is, in some ways, like E.M. Forster's Chandrapore in *A Passage to India*[3] — a deliberate, focused evocation — only more detailed and more heavily laced with irony.

In Mirpore, there are no alien rulers to exploit and plunder native resources. Yet, it is as decadent, neglected, and dying a town as Chandrapore:

> Although it lacked history, the town had probably existed for centuries in its most basic, most elemental form. Those shacks

of tin and rags, however precarious and impermanent they looked, must have existed always, repetitively and in succeeding generations, but never fundamentally changing and in that sense enduring. The roads that ran beween their crooked rows had been periodically laid down with tar but the dust beneath was always present, always perceptible. In fact, it managed to escape from under the asphalt and to rise and spread through the town, summer and winter, a constant presence, thick enough to be seen and felt. During the monsoon, always brief and disappointing on this northern plain more than a thousand miles from the coast, it turned to mud. But the sun came out again very soon and dried it to its usual grey and granular form. The citizens of Mirpore, petty tradesmen rather than agriculturists, could not be blamed for failing to understand those patriotic songs and slogans about the soil, the earth. To them it was so palpably dust. (p.19)

The passive resignation of Chandrapore's "inhabitants of mud" becomes here the cynicism and disillusionment of the citizens (note, they are referred to as "citizens" and not as "inhabitants") of Mirpore, the commercial city of "dust". Dust with its connotations of unproductivity, sterility, and death is more real to them than soil with its associations of vitality, creativity, growth. Throughout the novel, the nouns and adjectives that occur with almost uninterrupted regularity in the characterization of Mirpore are "debris", "desolation", "empty", "barren", "stagnant", "stale", "blight", "dustbin".

Mirpore is a town spoiled and neglected by its own citizens who seem to have no sense of history. There is no respect for monuments, no special signs or space or protection for them. The small mosque of marble and pink sandstone, built by a Nawab to commemorate his escape to this "obscure and thankfully forgotten town" after the revolt of 1857, and also to raise a memorial to the grace of God who had made his escape possible, was now

> so overgrown by the shacks, signboards, stalls, booths, rags, banners, debris and homeless poor of the bazaars that it would have been difficult for anyone to discern it beneath this multi-layered covering. Its white marble facings had turned grey and pock-marked through urban pollution, the black marble inlay

had either fallen out or been picked out by sharp instruments held in idle hands, the red sandstone of the dome had turned to the colour of filth from the smoke of open fires, the excreta of pigeons, and the ubiquitous dust of Mirpore. (p.20)

Of course, the traditional use of the mosque continued and five times a day the priest gave a call to worshippers and they came and prayed. But no one remembered it was a historical landmark nor attempted to reconstruct or restore it.

In other ways too, the town is the very essence of sterility. In the passage below, heavy irony is employed to suggest aridity and stagnation and the underlying despair and futility that mark the town:

Lacking a river, the town had an artificial tank in which people bathed and from which they fetched water although there was no water to be seen in it, only a covering layer of bright green scum on which bits of paper, rags and flowers rested as on a solid surface. There were wells, too, in which the water was even more successfully concealed. Mirpore spared no effort to give an impression of total aridity. (p.21)

In *A Passage To India*, Aziz had asked Fielding/the British to go — "Clear out, you fellows, double quick, I say" — so that India could become a nation of brothers:

India shall be a nation. No foreigners of any sort! Hindu and Moslem and Sikh and all shall be one! Hurrah! Hurrah for India! Hurrah! Hurrah! (p.317)

But in Mirpore in free India, the same communal divisions as under the British persist: "the area around the mosque was considered the 'Muslim' area and the rest 'Hindu'" (p.21). Although no boundaries marked one area from another there were differences between them, not easily discernible but known to all so that "pigs were generally kept out of the vicinity of the mosque and cows never slaughtered near a temple" (p.21). Even so, if once a year, Moharram and Holi happened to coincide, communal disturbances would break out and tensions remained high for a while. "Then the dust of Mirpore rose and swirled and buried everything in sight again; the citizens of Mirpore returned to their daily struggle to breathe" (pp.21-22).

Also to be found in Desai's Mirpore is the same fear of the Muslim of getting swamped by the dominant group, the same seeking of identity in the past days of glory and grand style of the Nawabs and in the use of the Urdu language — the language of the court, in the days of royalty, that had to be saved from being swallowed by that "vegetable monster, Hindi".

Mirpore has also had its share of 'development' — schools, colleges, the railway station, the bus terminus. Being close to Delhi, the busy centre of business and commerce, it always seemed to be in a state of "perpetual motion". However the bustle was strangely unproductive:

> the yellow sweets were amongst the very few things that were actually manufactured here; there was no construction to speak of, except the daily one of repairing; no growth except in numbers, no making permanent what had remained through the centuries so stubbornly temporary — and it was other cities, other places that saw the fruits of all the bustle, leaving the debris and the litter behind for Mirpore. (p.23)

The incantatory, irony-laden negations of worth, growth and creativity — "no construction... except the daily one of repairing", "no growth except in numbers", "no making permanent what had remained ... so stubbornly temporary" — build up Mirpore as a town with a miserable zero for its reason for existence.

However, besides the imaging of Mirpore, the novel is also about people, about human beings who entertain hopes and aspirations like people everywhere in the world. These are people who live both in that "prison", "trap", "dustbin", (as Mirpore is variously called by the characters in the book) and outside it, in Delhi, where some of the action in the book takes place.

First, there is Deven, the protagonist, a lecturer in Lala Ram Lal College, living in Mirpore with his wife, Sarla, and his son, Manu. Deven is the portrait of an ordinary, average human being. A lecturer in Hindi, he regards himself as a failure — both as a teacher and as someone who had unsuccessfully aspired to some status in life. At thirty-five he feels old already, having spent all the "empty years" waiting for a break, waiting to do something worthwhile, something "great". Deven is a romantic and an escapist, a weak person, incapable of facing crises. Unable to change his "circumstances", he seeks relief in fantasy and in the rich promises of Urdu poetry.

Sarla, his wife, is a "plain, penny-pinching, congenitally pessimistic" woman who had been selected by Deven's aunt as a bride for him for these very virtues. As a young girl and as a bride, she had the usual aspirations of her girl friends, to own the three F's — "'Fan, phone, frigidaire!' they would shout whenever anyone mentioned a wedding, a bridegroom, a betrothal, and dissolve in hectic laughter" (p.67). But by marrying into the academic profession and by living in a small town, all her dreams had been rudely swept away:

> The thwarting of her aspirations had cut two dark furrows from the corners of her nostrils to the corners of her mouth, as deep and permanent as surgical scars... They made her look forbidding, and perhaps that was why her husband looked so perpetually forbidden, even if he understood their cause. He understood because, like her, he had been defeated too; like her, he was a victim. (p.67)

Disappointment, however, had not brought them any closer. To live on a lecturer's salary can be an oppressive experience and though Deven and Sarla have no choice, it has given their marriage a permanent quality of despair.

A contrast to "thrifty", "domesticated" Deven is Siddiqui, his colleague, a Muslim lecturer in Urdu, a bachelor, a hedonist and a romantic who has the "talent for remaking fact into more acceptable, more attractive fiction". Thus, when he discovers that he can't make ends meet or maintain the disintegrating old *haveli*, his ancestral home, he sells it off to a Delhi businessman who wants to "develop" that land — build a block of flats with shops on the ground floor, a cinema house at the back, offices on top — "all kinds of plans for putting his wasteland to use".

Yet another contrast to Deven is Murad, his childhood friend, now in Delhi. To Deven, Murad, the son of a wealthy Kashmiri carpet seller, had been the rich spoilt boy with lots of money to spend on films and cigarettes while Deven had been a poor widow's son "who could be bribed and bought to do anything for him". Yet their friendship had stood the test of time. Murad is the editor of an Urdu journal which he says he runs to save the glorious traditions of Urdu from being extinguished by the Hindi-wallahs. He is probably not very rich now — he says that his father has disinherited him. Unlike Deven, he is resourceful and aggressive and seems to give the impression that he can have his way with most people. Even so, there is something quite pitiable about his attempts to get things out of people and maintain an appearance of decent living.

The motif of despair, failure, and mediocrity that underlines the lives of each of these people is repeated in several situations in the book — in the kind of homes, D/II type, that Deven and other low-paid employees in the same grade live in (p.71); in the alienating colonial system of education mirrored in the set-up of Lala Ram Lal College, Mirpore; in the attempts to teach the languages in a scene dominated by science studies; in the phenomenon of "braindrain" and migration to more prosperous countries for lucrative jobs and other "goodies" (pp.185-6).

What brings a dramatic change into the monotonous, purposeless existence of the protagonist, Deven — and by ripple effect, into the lives of some others — is a chance visit by Murad. His visit triggers off a chain of events from which Deven finds it difficult to extricate himself. Murad asks Deven to go to Delhi and interview Nur Shahjehanabadi, the greatest living Urdu poet of Delhi — though no longer very active — and to write an article for a special number he proposes to bring out on the poet.

For Deven, lover of Urdu poetry and admirer of Nur (as he is called), this becomes *the* very summons he has been waiting for all these years. In being asked to interview Nur, his idol since childhood, he feels that he has been "allotted a role in life". His first meeting with the poet is rather comic:

> Before he could make out who had opened the door and now stood behind it, he heard an immense voice, cracked and hoarse and thorny, boom from somewhere high above their heads: 'Who is it that disturbs the sleep of the aged at this hour of the afternoon that is given to rest? It can only be a great fool. Fool, are you a fool?'
> And Deven, feeling some taut membrane of reservation tear apart inside him and a surging expansion of joy at hearing the

voice and the words that could only belong to that superior being, the poet, sang back, 'Sir, I am! I am!'

There was an interval and then some mutters of astonishment and horror at this admission. In that quiet pause, pigeons were heard to gurgle and flutter as if in warning from the wings. (pp.38-9)

The mocking tone of the narrative places both Nur and Deven within a corrected perspective — Nur is no God, nor is Deven a fool or a court jester — but for a few moments in the drama of their meeting, everybody else is forced to occupy the wings of the stage while the "superior being" Nur and the nervous admirer and devotee, Deven, meet.

To be a success has always been an anxiety with Deven, and the meeting with Nur, once a fiery symbol of Urdu literary creation, the epitome of success, represents for Deven all that he could not be. Nur, in that sense, is Deven's *alter ego*. In the interview that Deven hopes to have with Nur, he really aspires to experience the bright promises of poetry as against the grey shades of his own incomplete existence. But Nur is already old and has lost much of his creativity at the time of the meeting, although Deven, blinded by his own adulation of the poet and his need to experience greatness and fame through him, refuses to accept this fact. In this self-deception lies much of Deven's later misery and the seeds of Nur's decision to exploit him. In fact, at the first meeting itself, Nur identifies him as a possible future victim:

> A wrinkled eyelid moved, like a turtle's, and a small, *quick eye* peered out at Deven as if at a *tasty fly*. (p.42; emphasis mine.)

Deven is manipulated very cleverly by Nur in a series of episodes that follow this meeting, the promised interview and the set of new couplets being dangled before him as a bait. In the hope of getting the poems and the interview, Deven allows himself to be cheated and befooled, his sincerity mocked at and held up for ridicule. In the last chapter of the book, Deven, now deserted by both Murad and Siddiqui, faces the prospect of a dismissal from his college for not having been able to procure the promised interview. In order to help Deven (with the expenses incurred in interviewing Nur), Siddiqui had earlier persuaded the college to buy a tape recorder and pay Nur's fee, on the ground that the tapes would be a valuable accretion to the library holdings of the Urdu department.

Besides, there is also the other matter of his understanding about the relationship between art and life. Having always held poetry to be superior to reality, Deven's concepts about poetry are rudely shaken when he is allowed into the poet's home with all its private and public moments. As one trying to record Nur's life and poetry, he wants only the poet, the creator, purged of all the dross of his life as a human being. But Nur comes to him with all the sordidness of his personal life — his poverty, age, parasitical companions, vulturish family — and his poetry. Deven's perpetual dilemma is how to sift Nur's art from Nur's life. Even in the secluded room Deven rents for recording only Nur's art, Nur comes with his noisy, loutish companions. And when Nur speaks, he rambles a lot, about *biryani*, rum and tales of a neighbour who once tried to rob him of two rupees — matters utterly unconnected with art, according to Deven.

The recording sessions, naturally, are a fiasco. Nur is temperamental, garrulous, but rarely talks of poetry. Furthermore, Deven's inefficient assistant seems to record only the irrelevant portions of Nur's discourses and to somehow miss out moments when Nur had talked of poetry. Nur, suddenly tired of the sessions, which have already lasted over three weeks, abandons Deven and refuses to talk or be recorded. Dispirited, Deven returns to Mirpore and faces the possibility of dismissal from his college. He who had yearned for a life away from the ordinary, now prays for the security of routine. Nur continues to send him one pathetic letter after another, begging him for money on some pretext or the other — his pigeons were dying and needed medicines; rent for the room where the recording was done; money to go to Mecca on his last pilgrimage, and so on. Deven does not reply to his letters.

Two important realizations then come to him out of his experiences. The first realization has to do with the central vision of the book and its title, *In Custody*: in taking somebody into custody, one has also to surrender oneself to the other's custody. To be merely custodian is to possess without being possessed and is a relationship of power. Both the epigraph and the conclusion of the novel suggest the need to recognize that every true relationship is essentially a two-way commitment, an act of continued responsibility for the other. Thus it is between true friends, between husband and wife, between artist and art, between art and the critic, between a person and his country, city, monuments. One does not abandon what one has once made use of:

> Deven had accepted the gift of Nur's poetry and that meant he was custodian of Nur's very soul and spirit. It was a great distinction. He could not deny or abandon that under any pressure. (p.204)

This realization in Deven, who had never willingly accepted responsibility, is indicative of his growth as a human being. It is a realization that the novel has been moving towards from the outset. In fact the novel's structure mirrors this movement. Unlike most novels that work towards one point of intensity or climax from which they finally return in a resolution, there are in this novel two focal points or peaks. One occurs at the end of chapter three, on Deven's first visit to Nur. Nur has retched after consuming a lot of drink and is being scolded by his second wife, the flamboyant Imtiaz Begum. Thoroughly shaken by this sordid episode that involves his idol, Deven abandons the poet and runs out of the house:

> Those were the two moments of the evening that stayed... the moment when he had stood above the well of the courtyard, listening to the voices inside, and the moment he had erupted out of the house, dropped the papers and run. What exactly had happened in between? There were times when he remembered a totally different scene: how he had marched in and thrust away the vengeful figure of a white and silver witch... but then his congenital inability to satisfy with fantasy would apply a brake ... and he would be faced with that one truth again — how he had abandoned the poet in his agony, desecrated the paper on which he wrote his verse, and run... (p.62)

The other occurs at the end of chapter nine, when the poet suddenly refuses to continue with the recording sessions:

> 'No, I will not resume,' Nur told him, shaking his head and continuing to shake it as he was led up the lane to the back door

of his house, Deven following in an agitated dance. Adamant up to the very door, he said, 'All one can resume, at my age, is the primordial sleep. I am going to curl up on my bed like a child in its mother's womb and I shall sleep, shall wait for sleep to come.'

The door in the wall opened and the servant boy helped him over the threshold and led him in. The door shut. (p.169)

In the first instance, it is Deven who abandons the poet, while in the second, it is the poet who abandons Deven and both focal points draw even. It is in chapter eleven, the last chapter, that the resolution occurs — when it dawns upon Deven that having taken something from each other once, neither could abandon the other. In giving him custody of his work, Nur in turn had earned the right to become Deven's custodian. Nur, therefore, could make demands on Deven — not only during his lifetime but also after his death, for his widows and his sons — and Deven would have to fulfil those demands. In vowing commitment, Deven discovers his identity and worth.

The second realization is that art is not separable from life. It is of the very stuff of life with all its ordinary, meaningless, routine acts. Art is like the recordings of Nur's short recitations interspersed with large rambling accounts of his favourite foods, and the blaring of car horns from the street below. Art is both the poem and the poet's vomit. (This has a reference to Imtiaz Begum bullying Deven into wiping the poet's vomit after he had retched. It was only as Deven was trying to discard the soiled sheets that he realized that they could have been Nur's poems.) Unlike Deven, Nur the true poet, had understood the problem of creativity very well. When Deven feels irritated at the recording sessions, and is unable to decide what to record and what to omit, Nur asks him:

'Has this dilemma come to you too then? This sifting and selecting from the debris of our lives? It can't be done, my friend, it can't be done. I learnt that long ago...' (p.167)

The technique of the novel reiterates this truth as well. Throughout the novel, verse — Nur's or that of the Romantics, Keats and Shelley — is subtly interspersed with descriptions of ordinary day-to-day existence, conflicts and problems.

Art, Deven realizes eventually, is like a perfect bubble, like the dome of the mosque in Mirpore: if one tries to dissolve art into life's problems and their answers, as one does in the sciences, then "the bubble would be breached and burst, and it would no longer be perfect". And if it were not perfect, then it would no longer be art (p.192).

Similarly, art cannot be split into life fit for art and life not fit for art. All of life has to go into art, whether it is unimaginative Mirpore or Deven's mediocre existence as husband, father, teacher. The creative exists within the routine, the derelict, the wretched. Life has to be accepted whole, as a package — the creative tangled hopelessly with the uncreative. The novel here acquires universal tones as it reverberates with meaning for the meaningless act of existence.

Reality is always depressing but the answer does not lie in escapist measures such as fantasizing about great deeds, or in migration — the fantasy of some of Deven's colleagues (pp.185-6) about remaking their future in more prosperous and "creative" countries — but in confronting reality headlong as it unfolds, unfettered by weak or cowardly thoughts. Deven learns this truth at the very end and is at peace with himself, at last:

> He walked up the path. Soon the sun would be up and blazing. The day would begin, with its calamities. They would flash out of the sky and cut him down like swords. He would run to meet them. He ran, stopping only to pull a branch of thorns from under his foot. (p.204)

The book has moments of humour — the comic and the mock heroic as in the passage cited above — and these work to defuse and edit the gravity with which the characters (being human after all) are prone to take events and happenings that do not match their expectations. In this respect, the novel is a bit like the novels of R.K. Narayan where events are always viewed from a comic perspective often to suggest that the characters have taken their problems far too seriously than was called for. In this context, I feel that Desai's *In Custody* is different from her other novels. Although the pervading philosophy in the novel is not similar to Narayan's (his is more in the traditional, Hindu metaphysical strain while hers is for a life that has to be faced squarely, with courage, integrity and responsibility), the novel ends on a note of hope and optimism. It evokes, through creative language, structures and technique, an image of India that belies the impression of a "dead", "stagnant" India. *In Custody* offers an image of India that is full of hope and that transcends the superficial irritants that many Anglo-Indian novelists have referred to — the heat and dust of India. It is a beautiful novel by a great Indian woman writer.

NOTES

1. Anita Desai, *Voices in The City* (New Delhi: Orient Paperbacks, 1965; next edition, 1982).

2. Anita Desai, *In Custody* (London: Heinemann, 1984). All subsequent references are to this edition.

3. E.M. Forster, *A Passage To India* (Harmondsworth: Penguin Books Ltd., 1975; first edition, 1924).

NISSIM EZEKIEL

An image of India in Shouri Daniels' *A City of Children*

A City of Children[1] by Shouri Daniels is a novella which was published along with four short stories in 1985. It is set in a New Delhi college for women and its characters are academics, with domestic servants, peons and chowkidars thrown in. The Indian publishers describe the academics, not surprisingly as "the new rich men and women" and, again, as "upper class creatures". It follows, from this point of view that they are guilty of "pretence and vanity" which the novella exposes. It seems that in India if you are not a peasant or an industrial worker, if you do not live on the pavements or in hutment colonies, then obviously you are rich. And how can you be rich, even if you are only a college teacher, without also being pretentious and vain?

The author, fortunately, cannot be accused of the social naivete and ideological distortions which her Indian publishers have so grotesquely projected in their catalogue note on *A City of Children*. She is a serious literary artist of a high order, a critic and satirist of Indian life with a devastating sense of humour and a subtle feeling for human dilemmas and contradictions which are not, it is necessary to point out, confined to the Indian scene. The Indian reader may, of course, respond unfavourably to the image of Indian life reflected in the novel, starting with the title which damns Delhi as a city of children, and the very first paragraph from which I quote partially:

> The neighbour's servant hawked and gargled before dawn, his yogic exercise for the day. The man was a social cypher, but he

certainly managed to grate on frayed nerves every morning. It was no use complaining; there was no law, written or unwritten, against yoga. He shattered the peace of the morning before the cocks of the Thieves Colony across the street started their orisons.... Killer buses roared driven by demons and lorries had their cargoes of workmen who, like schoolboys on a picnic, waved and hooted as they kept their places in the crush of bodies.

I am sure some Indian readers will blame the character with the frayed nerves in the morning, rather than the neighbour's servant, and ask querulously what yoga has to do with his hawking and gargling. Cocks have been known to crow even in idyllic rural surroundings, and it is not only in India that buses are driven by demons. As for the workmen hooting in lorries, it only shows that our people are more natural and spontaneous, particularly when they are unspoilt by Westernized education, depicted in all its degenerate ways throughout the novel.

It is Sulochana Ravat, one of its products, who can't stand the noise of the place. She "experienced relative silence" only when she read the human interest stories in *The Hindustan Times*, and *The Times of India* for July 18. Scolded by his wife and assaulted for coming home late from work when their daughter is ill, the husband pours kerosene on himself and sets himself on fire. A woman was told by her mother-in-law that her children are bastards, "not my son's children," the old lady said. The young woman kills them. Sulochana asks herself, "Why am I so sympathetic to these people in the newspaper and unsympathetic to the people outside my window?" It is one of many questions in the novel to which neither the characters nor the author has any answers. But we remember the questions. And we cannot doubt the veracity of even the most minor asides about the novel's non-characters, so to speak, who appear briefly and disappear from the narrative. Mr. Kewal, for example, the kind of Head Clerk with whom we are all familiar.

> He was long-winded. He qualified. He evaded. He created extra work in his office of nineteen clerks and typists, all male. He also fought protracted battles of little consequence with Mr. Gopali, the South Indian accountant. He was feared by the

Class Four employees, eleven gardeners, four sweepers, thirty chaprasis, two chowkidars, all male — but for the sweeper woman. He was the supreme authority and legislator for fifty people under him. Like the god in the temple, he received their special offerings of sweets, and garlands on festive occasions. On his desk was a large board facing the visitor which said in white on ebony, "Please be brief." Actually, it ought to have been facing him, not the visitor. It is said of him that rancid butter would turn into crystals in his mouth at the sight of the Principal, Dr. Bolar. (p.11)

In masterly control of her material, Shouri Daniels waits for the third chapter of the seventeen of her novella before she introduces the Black Doll. Its presence in the college is reported, appropriately, by the watchman, Sunderlal, to Chinna Verma who is in dubious telepathic communication with the woman mystic Jayshree Mai. Chinna's new maid from Madras is suspected by the watchman, Sunderlal, to be the same one who had been sent to prison ten years earlier by Sulochana Ravat, "in mysterious circumstances" needless to say. Chinna's aunt's butler, on the other hand, claimed that the girl had never left home. He didn't want her to be sent out on errands and so on, convinced that "Delhi was full of dangers for a well-brought-up girl from Madras". Chinna broods over the notion : "Being a virgin was equated with being good", she reflects, though in her own case, being unmarried, she wishes, or perhaps Shouri Daniels wishes for her, that someone would take her virginity.

The Black Doll, according to the legend, made anyone who owned it "sought after overnight" and they could then "pick and choose any man they wanted". It sounds as much an Indian legend as that equation between gargling and yoga. The whole of chapter three, which is one of the longest in the novella, is devoted to Chinna's thoughts about what it means to be a woman, about virginity, sex and a bawdy story, the meaning of which, at twenty five, she was considered too young to know. The bawdiness, not only in this chapter but whenever it rears its ugly whatever throughout the novella, is sinister in its meaningfulness. But I need not quote examples. What matters is that it matters, like a secret that is no longer available only to a few but to everybody. And the humour is both quite commonplace and very special, as when Meena reporting her advice to Biku, to tighten up at the right moment and it works, is interrupted by a man's voice, "I yam from the Sharma College for Men. I yam Gupta from the Math Department", which is only routine Indian English pronunciation, but then a joke is never merely a joke in *A City of Children*. It can be interpreted as a slogan, which I-yam-Gupta does. "Tighten up, it works! Tighten up, it works!" When the women hear Gupta say this, they look, the author tells us, "as if they had been shot at close range". But whatever happens, they believe in the Black Doll and in the necessity of belief to break the cycle of doubt. The one who doesn't share this dogma is the Parsee Biku who seems to announce the author's conviction: "The world belongs to the educated woman. No one needs witchcraft to find a mate." The author's mini-portrait of Biku, who has known marriage and divorce, at the end of the chapter, with a characteristic direct comment on it as narrator, is also worth noting:

> Biku felt that she had survived unscathed because she did not court intensity, perversity, morbidity, or originality. These were the real dangers facing some of the younger women she knew. Ambition had stung them, and they would do anything to be counted different. She believed in old notions, and that there was 'a proper way' of doing each thing. She had a clock in every room and she had never been untidy in the years that she was at Narang. The pleats of her saris fell gracefully, she wore pastel colours that went with her Persian complexion. She looked like one of the women painted on mirrors in Irani restaurants in Bombay as in art-deco pictures. Rossetti was her favourite poet. If she knew a little more about the lives of the pre-Raphaelites, she would not have been entranced by their art. (pp. 36-37)

The passage could be analyzed to assess the author's strength or weaknesses in relation to the character analyzed. One wonders about that clock in every room and about the lives of the pre-Raphaelites. But the comparison with the women painted on mirrors in Bombay's Irani restaurants is just right.

The surprises never end in *A City of Children*; no chapter begins in a predictable way, nor does any episode follow the pattern laid down by the real or apparent demands of the narrative. A drug experience of Meenakshi's is covered as if it is the author's, who is certainly at home with nightmares as with a husband. The topical enters the picture directly from time to time, as does, for example, President Rajendra Prasad's guru, living in a picturesque ruin. He turns out to be the king of the Thieves Colony. The routine problems of Indian women, the sexual infidelities and the ambiguous relationships among the academics are presented as though they are scenes from the author's private diary. So even when an event moves away from the novella's normal realism to fantasy, it puts no strain on the author's credibility. The stories about the Black Doll no doubt belong to the realm of fantasy but are given some fine touches of real life as well. Shona, after acquiring the Doll, not only got married but was taken on a world tour by her hotelier husband. She passed the Doll on to a slim boyish girl from U.P., who rode a Lambretta, cut her hair short, and had lost her virginity, so she had no prospect of getting married. Thanks to the Black Doll, she not only got married, but had her virginity restored! The pimply girl who got that Doll next received an offer of marriage from an under-secretary in the Ministry of Defence. The combination of fantasy and humour with a secure base in commonplace Indian life is generally successful in *A City of Children*.

I shall resist the temptation to mention more of the funny (and always meaningful) elements in the novella. We do sometimes feel that the fiction is excessively fictional, but then the point of such excesses has been appreciated since contemporary Latin American writers appeared on the international scene during recent decades. Miss Basu, after some talk about the Black Doll with Miss Ghosh and Mrs Meenakshi, "felt as if she were a transient at a hostel for characters from fiction". We, the readers, feel the same.

It is the same with some of the recurring themes, such as infidelity. In the case of the College Principal's husband, it assumes enormous proportions. He keeps boxes of notes on various women, his excuse being that he was a sociologist by training. He was even "interested" in a servant girl who took to "putting flowers in her hair and posing in doorways like the women in Bombay's red-light district". The butler got rid of her, but our sociologist doesn't even mention the girl's sudden absence. A gap can always be filled. "There were so many gaps," comments the author, "so many new interests." There is a scandal at the end, and a double death, the second that of Sulochana

Ravat. She kills herself because, after her husband's suicide, her continued existence is intolerable to those around her, students, teachers, everyone. The Black Doll in Indian life wins over the author's irony and humour, the pleasant as well as the unpleasant realities, the fantasy and the crucial ambiguities of the narrative.

NOTES

1. Shouri Daniels, *A City of Children* (Delhi: Chanakya Publications, 1985). All subsequent references are to this edition.

Index

Achebe, Chinua, 18
Alice in Wonderland, 100
All My Sons, 58
Amur, G.S., 20n
Anand, Mulk Raj, 4, 13, 19
Andersen, Hans Christian, 89
Anita Desai, 50n, 101n
Anita Desai the Novelist, 101n
Apprentice, The, 51-60
Area of Darkness, An, 20n
Asnani, Shyam N., 49n
Aurobindo, Sri, 1

Bachelor of Arts, The, 67n
Badve, V.V., 79, 83n
Bannerjee, S.N., 1
Bend in the Ganges, A, 12
Beyond Culture, 67n
Bhagavadgita, The, 6, 35, 88, 89, 90
Bhave, Vinoba, 82
Blackmur, R.P., 39, 50n
Brahmo Samaj, 1
Buddha, 34
Bye Bye Blackbird, 36-50

Camus, Albert, 67, 67n
Cat and Shakespeare, The, 69
Chaitanya, Krishna, 50n
Chandrabhaga, 50

Chattopadhyaya, Virendranath, 81
Chessmaster and his Moves, The, 69
City of Children, A, 135-140
Clear Light of Day, 102-112
Cocktail Party, The, 91n
Coleridge, Samuel, 50
Collected Works of Lenin, 81
Commonwealth Quarterly, 83n
Complete Poems and Plays of T.S. Eliot, 91n
Comrade Kirillov, 69-83
Confucius 18
Conrad, Joseph, 54
Corbett, Jim, 14
Contemporary Indian Literature, 49n
Cry the Peacock, 38

Dark Dancer, The, 90
Das, Manas Mukul, 50n
De, S.K., 90, 91n
Derrett, M.E., 42, 50n
Desai, Anita, 36, 37, 38, 41, 49, 50n, 92, 98, 99, 100, 101, 101n, 102, 103, 104, 105, 107, 108, 109, 111, 112n, 123, 126, 133, 134n
Desani, G.V., 19
Desai, S.K., 20
Dey, Esha, 79, 83n

Index

Distant Drum, 14-15
Dostoevsky, Fyodor, 70, 79

Eliot, T.S., 89, 91n
Elizabeth, Queen, 8
Essays on Indian Writing in English, 20n

Fear of Freedom, The, 37
Financial Expert, The, 55, 60n, 68n
Fire on the Mountain, 92-101
Foreigner, The, 44, 53
Forster, E.M., 123, 134n
Fromm, Erich, 37, 38, 44, 47, 50n

Gandhi, Indira, 115, 117
Gandhi, M.K., 5, 14, 18, 54, 71, 77, 79, 82, 117
Gasset, Ortega y, 45
Gods, Demons and Others, 67n
Gokhale, G.K., 1
Greene, Graham, 67, 68n
Guide, The, 63, 65

Hamlet, 109
Higden, David Leon, 100, 101n
Highroads Treasury, 15
Hindu, The, 49n
Hindustan Times, The, 136
History of the Freedom Movement in India, 76, 83n
Hitler, Adolf, 5, 72, 73, 74

Illustrated Weekly of India, The, 83n
In Custody, 123-134
India: A Wounded Civilization, 67n
Indian Fiction in English, 91n
Indian Journal of English Studies, The, 83n
Indian Writing in English, 19, 20n
Inside the Haveli, 84-91
Iyengar, K.R. Srinivas, 19, 20n, 38

Jinnah, Mohammad Ali, 119

Joshi, Arun, 51, 52, 53, 59n
Journal of Commonwealth Literature, 83n
Journal of Indian Writing in English, The, 34n
Journal of South Asian Literature, 49n

Kafka, Franz, 40
Kanthapura, 69
Keats, John, 132
Khan, Yahya, 117
Khankhoje, P., 81
Kirkpatrick, Joanna, 36, 39n
Krishnan, S., 67n
Krishna Menon, V.K., 79, 80
Krishnamurti, J., 79

Lenin, V.I., 5, 6, 72, 81
Lion and the Honeycomb, The, 50n
Littcritt, 83n
Literary Endeavour, The, 67n
Luganin, G.A., 81

Mahabharata, The, 91n
Majumdar, R.C., 63, 76, 83n
Major Indian Novels, 101n
Malgonkar, Manohar, 12, 13, 14, 18, 19, 20
Man-eaters of Kumaon, 14
Manusmriti, 86
Markandaya, Kamala, 21, 34n
Marx, Karl, 5, 9, 72
Meditations on Quixote, 45
Mehta, Rama, 84, 91n
Midnight's Children, 113-122
Miller, Arthur, 58
Modernity and Contemporary Literature, 50n
Modern Indian Novel in English, The, 50n
Mozart, Wolfgang Amadeus, 110
Mr. Sampath, 67
Mukherjee, Meenakshi, 20, 20n, 91n

Index

Naidu, Sarojini, 81
Naik, M.K., 20, 20n, 71, 80, 83n, 101n
Naipaul, V.S., 18, 19, 20n, 66, 67n
Nandakumar, Prema, 101n
Narasimhaiah, C.D., 20, 20n
Narayan, R.K., 10, 19, 55, 61, 62, 63, 65, 66, 67n, 133
Nehru, Jawaharlal, 5, 115
New Pelican Guide to English Literature, The, 122n
New Quest, 83n
Nightingale, Florence, 66
Nowhere Man, The, 21, 45

Painter of Signs, The, 61-68
Passage to India, A, 48, 123, 125, 134n
Perspectives on Anita Desai, 112n
Perspectives on Indian Fiction in English, 101n
Phule, Jyotiba, 1
Possessed, The, 70, 79, 81
Possession, 21-35
Prasad, Hari Mohan, 49, 50
Prasad, Madhusudhan, 101n
Princes, The, 12-20
Psychology of Freedom, The, 50n

Radhakrishnan, S., 34
Raja Rao, 83n
Rajan, B., 90
Rajan, P.K., 83n
Rao, Raja, 1, 2, 4, 5, 10, 11, 19, 69, 70, 71, 72, 76, 77, 78, 79, 80, 81, 82, 83n
Rao, Vimala, 65, 67n
Ranade, M.G., 1
Ray, Satyajit, 4
Rebel, The, 67n
Rhetoric of Literary Character, A, 50n
Roy, M.N., 79, 80
Roy, Rammohan, 1, 82
Rushdie, Salman, 19, 113, 120, 122n
Russell, Bertrand, 15

Sane Society, The, 41, 50
Saratchandra, 4
Second Coming, The, 12
Sen Gupta, Ranjana, 49n
Serpent and the Rope, The, 1-11, 69, 70, 79
Sethi, Sunil, 112n
Shakespeare, William, 8
Shankaracharya, 24
Sharma, K.K., 11n
Sharma, R.S., 50n, 101n
Shelley, P.B., 116
Shepherd, Ron, 10, 10n
Shourie, Arun, 83n
Some Inner Fury, 21
Span, 67n
Spencer, Dorothy M., 91n
Springer, Mary Doyle, 48, 50n
Srivastava, Narasingh, 79, 83n
Srivastava, Ramesh, 112
Stalin, Josef, 5, 7, 8, 72, 73, 74, 75, 76, 77
Strange Case of Billy Biswas, The, 54
Swan and the Eagle, The, 20, 20n
Syed Amanuddin, 21, 34n

Things Fall Apart, 18
Times Literary Supplement, The, 18, 19, 20n
Tilak, B.G., 1
Trilling, Lionel, 61, 67n
Trotsky, Leon, 5, 6, 7, 8
Twice-Born Fiction, The, 20, 20n
Two Virgins, 21

Vendor of Sweets, The, 57
Victoria, Queen, 16
Vivekananda, Swami, 80
Voices in the City, 38, 123, 134n

Waiting for the Mahatma, 62

Yeats, W.B., 12
Youth, 54

E-mail
<raj@unipune.ernet.in>